# The Gospel of John
# in Christian History

# Theological Inquiries

## Studies in Contemporary
## Biblical and Theological Problems

General Editor
Rev. Lawrence Boadt, C.S.P.

PAULIST PRESS
New York • Ramsey • Toronto

# The Gospel of John in Christian History

*Essays for Interpreters*

J. Louis Martyn

Paulist Press
New York • Ramsey • Toronto
1978

ms: NT John — criticism, interpretation

Library of Congress
Catalog Card Number: 78-70821

ISBN: 0-8091-2170-0

Published by Paulist Press
*Editorial Office:* 1865 Broadway, New York, N.Y. 10023
*Business Office:* 545 Island Road, Ramsey, N.J. 07446

Printed and bound in the
United States of America

# Contents

# Preface

The chapters of this book have grown in several settings geographically far removed from one another, and in those settings a number of people have made substantive contributions to their growth. During a remarkable sabbatical year in Jerusalem, 1974-75, colleagues at the Ecumenical Institute and at the École Biblique offered themselves as generous conversation partners. In March 1975 the oral forms of Chapters 1 and 2 were given as guest lectures at the Universities of Amsterdam, Groningen, Leiden, and Utrecht; it is pleasant to recall the gracious and helpfully critical discussions with my Dutch hosts and colleagues, and with their students. The lecture form of Chapter 3 was proffered at the Journées Bibliques convened in August 1975 at Pope Adrian College in Louvain. On that occasion the discussion was extraordinarily lively, and the printed form now takes account of that discussion at several points. Similarly helpful responses were given to Chapter 2 when it was presented to colleagues of the Studiorum Novi Testamenti Societas in Aberdeen a few days later. And there are comparable debts to attentive auditors at the 1975 meeting of the Society of Biblical Literature in Chicago and at the 1976 summer lectures at Assumption College in Worcester, Massachusetts.

Originally conceived in relation to one another, the three studies have developed in ways which cause them to be even more closely intertwined. Since they have previously appeared in widely scattered publications, I am delighted that the present volume makes it possible to draw them together under a single cover. For this volume I have fundamentally rewritten Chapter 2, and I have throughout translated into English those texts which were earlier quoted in their original languages.

\*      \*      \*

Chapter 1 was published in R. Hammerton Kelly and R. Scroggs (eds.), *Jews, Greeks and Christians*, Essays in Honor of William David Davies (Leiden, 1976), pp. 181-219. In a rather more technical form Chapter 2 was originally written for J. Jervell and W. A. Meeks (eds.), *God's Christ and His People*, Essays Honoring Nils Alstrop Dahl (Oslo, 1977) under the title "Clementine Recognitions 1, 33-71, Jewish Christianity, and the Fourth Gospel." The third chapter was issued in M. de Jonge (ed.), *L'Évangile de Jean*, Sources, rédaction, théologie (*BETL* XLIV, Leuven, 1977), pp. 149-175. The editors of these Festschriften and of this congress volume have kindly supported the issuance of the present book.

# Introduction

During the last decades, studies in the Gospel of John have been moving at a remarkable pace. We have seen the appearance of several truly profound commentaries and a host of scientific monographs, a number of which have proven to be genuinely perceptive.[1] Significant strides have thus been made at perhaps half a dozen points, two of which merit special attention: the study of the Gospel's view of Christ (its christology) and attempts to ascertain the Gospel's portrait of the Church (its ecclesiology). Indeed these two areas stand out, not only because important work has been done in them, but also because some of the work that has been done is of such a nature as to give strong hints regarding what the next steps might be. It is primarily for these reasons that the present volume is designed to explore both Johannine christology and Johannine ecclesiology.

## CHRISTOLOGY

The reader of John's Gospel will not have proceeded eighteen verses into the first chapter without sensing the massive concentration of the author's attention on christology. It is immediately understandable that numerous interpreters have pointed to christology as the evangelist's central interest. But centrality is surely

---

[1] See the commentaries by R. E. Brown, R. Schnackenburg, B. Lindars, and (in a revised edition) C. K. Barrett. A vast number of monographs have been touched upon by Robert Kysar, *The Fourth Evangelist and His Gospel* (Augsburg, 1975). See also M. de Jonge (ed.), *L'Evangile de Jean, Sources rédaction, théologie* (Louvain, 1977), and the articles in *Interpretation* 31 (1977) no. 4

too weak an image. For in the work of this author, as Ernst Käsemann has recently put it, christology constitutes the whole of the horizon, with the result that other matters such as pneumatology, eschatology, and ecclesiology find their supporting positions at discrete points, so to speak, along the christological horizon.[2]

As regards exegetical research directed to this remarkable christology, the scholarly clock has not been standing still. Were one to reread the pages on John's christology in Wilhelm Bousset's justly famous *Kyrios Christos* immediately before perusing the major contributions of the last two decades, one would see that solid advances have been made on the basis of the hypothesis that to a large degree the christological formulations of this Gospel are derived from concepts originally at home in streams of Jewish thought. Writing almost three quarters of a century ago, Bousset concluded that the titles "Son of Man" and "Kyrios" were of Jewish and Gentile Hellenistic derivation respectively, and he assumed with many of his contemporaries that John's Gospel lay in the line of the post-Pauline Gentile Hellenistic Church, in which the latter title had all but eclipsed the former. When he turned to John's Gospel, Bousset was therefore greatly puzzled to find exactly what he did not expect: in this "Hellenistic Gospel" the "Gentile Christian" title "Kyrios" is virtually absent, while the "Jewish Christian" title "Son of Man" clearly stands very near the center of the proclamation about Jesus.[3] Being unable, one supposes, to question his historical scheme in a radical way, Bousset responded to the puzzle merely by formulating several "explanations" which have proven to be quite unpersuasive.

---

[2] Ernst Käsemann, *The Testament of Jesus* (Fortress, 1968), p. 16.

[3] Bousset's confidence that the title "Kyrios" was first used of Jesus in the Gentile Christian Church is shared by relatively few New Testament scholars today. See, e.g., R. H. Fuller, *The Foundations of New Testament Christology* (Scribner's, 1965), pp. 185f.; note also the weighty arguments of Ph. Vielhauer, "Ein Weg zur neutestamentlichen Christologie?" *EvTh* 25 (1965) 24-72, especially 28ff., and of J. A. Fitzmyer, "Der semitische Hintergrund des neutestamentlichen Kyriostitels," G. Strecker (ed.), *Jesus Christus in Historie und Theologie*, Festschrift Conzelmann (Tübingen, 1975), pp. 267-298.

Recent interpreters, following a rather different path, have noted not only the weighty influence on John of Jewish specula-tion about the Son of Man,[4] but also the extensive signs in the Gospel of the impact of Jewish wisdom traditions,[5] and the pow-erful effect on John's christology of Jewish thought patterns fo-cused on Moses.[6] Such discoveries have gone a long way toward clarifying the conceptual background of the Gospel's christology.

It is important to notice, however, that these solid advances have not answered the whole of Bousset's puzzle. As I have just indicated, they tell us a great deal about the Gospel's *intellectual milieu*—it is far more Jewish than Bousset imagined—but they are not designed to address in a direct way the question which perplexed Bousset much more than that of the general intellectual milieu: Where does the Gospel of John belong within *the history of specifically Christian thought and life*? It follows—if one is convinced that Bousset's question remains essential for the fuller interpretative task—that Johannine exegetes cannot be satisfied indefinitely to move about in the realm of disembodied ideas—this one is quite "Jewish," that one is rather "Gnostic," etc. On the contrary, we have in fact to return to Bousset's passionate concern to fix the locus occupied by John in the history of early Christianity.

Where will such a move lead us? At the present juncture in Johannine research one would be wise to claim little more, I think, than a glimpse of the path opening up ahead. Recall that

---

[4] See the monograph of S. Schulz, *Untersuchungen zur Menschensohn-Christologie im Johannesevangelium* (Vandenhoeck und Ruprecht, 1957), the articles by S. Smalley, "The Johannine Son of Man Sayings," *NTS* 15 (1968-69), 278-301, E. Ruckstuhl, "Die johanneische Menschensohnforschung 1957-1969," *Theologische Berichte* 1 (1972) 171-284, and P. Borgen, "Some Jewish Exegetical Traditions as Back-ground for Son of Man Sayings in John's Gospel (John 3:13-14 and Context)," pp. 243-258 in M. de Jonge (ed.) *L'Évangile de Jean.*

[5] See notably R. E. Brown, *The Gospel According to John* (i-xii), The Anchor Bible, Vol. 29 (Doubleday, 1966) CXXII-CXXVII, and R. G. Hamerton-Kelly, *Pre-Existence, Wisdom, and the Son of Man* (Cambridge, 1973), pp. 197ff.

[6] W. A. Meeks, *The Prophet-King, Moses Traditions and the Johannine Christology* (Brill, 1967).

when Bousset referred to the title "Son of Man," he was speaking in the first instance not of a disembodied *Jewish idea*, but rather of a title widely employed by flesh-and-blood *Jewish Christians* in their cultic life. It may follow that in ways he never dreamed of we should reformulate Bousset's riddle by asking whether the Gospel of John could perhaps be far more closely related to Jewish Christianity than we have previously thought. In short, we may be able to make further headway by de-emphasizing for a brief period our quite legitimate concern with such conceptual adjectives as "Jewish" and "Gnostic," in order vigorously to focus our attention on such historical nouns as "Jewish Christianity" and "Gentile Christianity." The two approaches are, of course, far from being mutually exclusive. The point is simply that the former has been pursued quite productively in recent years, while the latter has been largely neglected.

It is along the path thus indicated that the initial essay in the present volume has emerged. What are we to say regarding the locus of John's christology along the multiple and complex lines of christological development in the early Church? Did the evangelist have discernible christological predecessors, and, if so, are we able with some specificity to discover the contours of their views of Christ? Assuming for the moment positive answers, we would then be in a position to ask how and why the evangelist handled the formulations of his predecessors as he did, thus arriving at the majestic christology which subsequent theologians have consistently recognized as peculiarly his own. I am quite sure that in a single essay I have not fully answered these demanding questions, but I hope to have taken a few constructive steps that may eventually help us more fully to perceive where and how John's christology fits into the history of christological patterns in early Christianity.

## ECCLESIOLOGY

The second part of the book, Chapters 2 and 3, consists of two further essays also concerned with the issue of John's place in the history of early Christianity. In these I have concentrated not on christology, but rather on ecclesiology in a manner which is quite concrete. Here I have asked myself several questions: In what kind of community did the evangelist live? What was it like to experience daily life in that community? And, finally, are we able to piece together at least a partial picture of the community's own history?

In the first of these essays my concern with such questions led me—for reasons I shall explain in a moment—into the labyrinth of the Pseudo-Clementine literature. (I have given a brief introduction to this literature early in the second chapter, and I have provided an English translation of the pertinent part of it in an appendix.) It may be salutary for me to say quite directly that I was myself surprised to find my interest directed toward those rather exotic and esoteric writings known more or less exclusively to scholars of patristics as the Clementine *Homilies* and *Recognitions*. More than one scholar has disappeared into the Pseudo-Clementine labyrinth never to be heard from again! Why not stick to the text of John's Gospel itself, or at the very least to the New Testament?

Again the major answer lies in the hypothesis that our Gospel may be much more closely connected with Jewish Christianity than we have previously thought. If so, we need for comparative purposes to look to those few documents of Jewish Christianity which survived the suppressive measures of orthodox censors, with an eye to the testing of our hypothesis. In this regard, relatively little is to be found in the New Testament itself. By and large, and with regard to the *present form*—the uppermost layers—of its writings, the New Testament is, as H.-J. Schoeps has remarked, a collection of the documents of the victorious party, the emerging Great Church.[7] But there is a discrete stratum of tradition in the fourth-century Pseudo-Clementine literature which has long been thought to preserve an extraordinarily valuable source for the study of one branch of early Jewish Christianity, and, unlikely as it may seem, a careful reading of this source in parallel, so to speak, with pertinent sections of the Gospel of John leads to the suggestion that at one stage in their

---

[7]H. J. Schoeps, *Jewish Christianity* (Fortress, 1969), p. 3.

respective histories the communities behind these two documents underwent some quite similar experiences precisely as Jewish-Christian communities. Comparison of the two communities thus leads, I think, to a clearer and more nearly complete picture of the fabric of their daily life.

The final essay is designed to draw together the major threads from the other studies and, indeed, from several previous publications as well.[8] As the title indicates, the intention is to present a sketch of the history of the Johannine community from its origin through the period of its life during which the Gospel of John was composed. Here several convictions are pursued, the chief ones being: (1) there are numerous literary strata behind the text of the Gospel as we have it; (2) to some extent it is possible to differentiate these strata from one another, thus discovering significant traces of the literary history behind the Gospel; (3) this literary history reflects to a large degree the history of a single community which maintained over a period of some duration its particular and rather peculiar identity.

It follows that we may hope to draw from the Gospel's literary history certain conclusions about the community's social and theological history. Broadly put, three major periods emerge:

1. The Early Period presumably began before the Jewish revolt and lasted until some point in the eighties. Our study of some of the lines of development which lie behind the evangelist's own majestic christology (Chapter 1 of the present book) helps us find our bearings as regards this early period. We see here a *group of Christian Jews* living in a stream of relatively untroubled theological and social continuity within the synagogue.

2. The Middle Period was ushered in when the remarkable growth of this group aroused the suspicions of the Jewish authorities and led them to take severely repressive steps designed to terminate what they saw as a serious threat. Such persecution caused some members of the group, and some who had been

---

[8]*History and Theology in the Fourth Gospel* (first edition, Harper and Row, 1968; revised edition to be published by Abingdon. 1979; "Source Criticism and Religionsgeschichte in the Fourth Gospel," *Jesus and Man's Hope* (Pittsburgh Seminary, 1970) I, 247-273.

attracted to it, to turn back from an open confession in order to remain safely in the synagogue. Those who made an open confession were excommunicated and thus became a *separated community of Jewish Christians* who were then subjected to further persecution (Chapter 2). The painful events of the Middle Period had lasting effects on the community's understanding both of Christ and of itself.

3. The Late Period saw further developments in the community's christology and ecclesiology, and it is now clear that these developments were worked out to a large extent vis-à-vis not only the parent synagogue, but also other Christian groups known to the Johannine community. Thus, when the Gospel found its final form, the horizon displayed at least four discrete social and theological groups:

1. The synagogue of "the Jews";
2. Christian Jews within the synagogue who attempted secretly to maintain a dual loyalty, and toward whom the Johannine community felt enormous antipathy;
3. The Johannine community itself;
4. Other communities of Jewish Christians who had also experienced expulsion from the synagogue, and with whom the Johannine community hoped eventually to be unified.

I say that the horizon displayed *at least* these four groups because I am sure that the situation was yet more complex; and indeed recent studies have begun further to expand and qualify this picture.[9] Such studies give me reason to hope that in the chapters

---

[9] Some of the major developments are appearing in recent articles by my colleague Raymond E. Brown: "Johannine Ecclesiology—The Community's Origins," *Interpretation* 31 (1977) 379-393; " 'Other Sheep Not of this Fold': The Johannine Perspective on Christian Diversity in the Late First Century," *JBL* 97 (1978), 5-22; "The Relationship to the Fourth Gospel Shared by the Author of I John and by His Opponents." Text and Interpretation: Studies Presented to Matthew Black (Cambridge, 1979). The picture which has been unfolding in these articles is

offered here an angle of vision may emerge in a way that is sufficiently constructive to be of help to other Johannine interpreters.

now brought together and further enriched in Raymond E. Brown, *The Community of the Beloved Disciple* (New York: Paulist Press, 1979). See also D. M. Smith, Jr., "Johannine Christianity: Some Reflections on Its Character and Delineation" *NTS* 21 (1974-1975) 222-248; R. A. Culpepper, *The Johannine School* (Scholars Press, 1975); O. Cullman, *The Johannine Circle* (Westminster, 1976); A. J. Mattill, "Johannine Communities Behind the Fourth Gospel: Georg Richter's Analysis," *TS* 38 (1977) 294-315; R. Schnackenburg, "Die johanneische Gemeinde und ihre Geisterfahrung," R. Schnackenburg, J. Ernst, and J. Wanke (eds.) *Die Kirche des Anfangs,* Festschrift für Heinz Schürmann zum 65, Geburtstag (Leipzig: St. Benno, 1977), pp. 277-306; F. Vouga, *Le cadre historique et l'intention théologigue de Jean* (Paris, 1977).

# CHAPTER 1

# "We Have Found Elijah"

**A View of Christ Formulated Very Early in the Life of the Johannine Community**

## I. A MODERN DEBATE

It is customary for authors of New Testament christologies to comment on the roles played in patterns of Jewish expectation by "the eschatological prophet," whether or not they consider the figure to be directly pertinent to christology as such.[10] Moreover there is general agreement that in first-century Judaism such patterns of expectation were primarily focused on two dominant figures, Moses and Elijah. The remarks of Cullmann are typical:

> The Jewish belief in a returning prophet took the particular form of an expectation of the return of a particular Old Testament prophet at the end of days. This expectation arises already with the words of Deut. 18:15 . . . [pointing to] the appearance of a prophet similar to [Moses]. . . . Above all, however, the return of Elijah was expected [as is attested in Malachi, Sirach, and rabbinical texts].[11]

---

[10] Examples include O. Cullmann, *The Christology of the New Testament* (London, 1959), pp. 13-50; F. Hahn, *The Titles of Jesus in Christology* (New York, 1969), where the matter is taken up in an appendix, pp. 352-406; and Fuller, *Foundations*, pp. 46-48, 67, 125-29, 167-73.

[11] Cullmann, *Christology*, pp. 16f.; cf. Hahn, *Titles*, p. 354; and Fuller, *Foundations*, pp. 46ff.

9

The distinguishing of these two forms of expectation from one another is clearly presupposed in two carefully worded statements of R. H. Fuller:

> The early Aramaic speaking church interpreted Jesus' earthly ministry explicitly in terms of the Mosaic prophet servant. The primary evidence for this is . . . the Petrine speech (Acts 3:12-26). . . . [However] there is no evidence that the post-Easter church ever interpreted Jesus . . . as Elijah *redivivus*, although certain traits from the Elijah traditions were taken up into the later conception of Jesus as an eschatological prophet. Rather, in Christian tradition John the Baptist himself became Elijah *redivivus* (Mark 9:13).[12]

Essentially the same position is taken by F. Hahn:

> There is a series of indications that the idea of the eschatological prophet was carried over to Jesus and that this was apparently done very early. . . . Here we are concerned *throughout* [durchweg] with the type of expectation that bears upon it the stamp of Deut. 18:15ff. (Footnote: On the basis of Mk. 6:15; 8:18 the question could be asked whether Jesus was not actually also regarded as the eschatological Elias. . . . It may not on any account be disputed that *a whole series of traits* remind us of Elias, but this is not the prevailing conception; rather we are clearly concerned here with separate *elements which were taken up into that other view* [the Mosaic one] of Jesus as the eschatological prophet. . . . This is easy to understand for the reason that . . . the Baptist community had already taken over the Elias conception.)[13]

To put it in a single sentence: The earliest Church viewed the Baptist as Elijah; that being the case, while some Elijah-like traits attached themselves to (the Mosaic portrait of) Jesus, *there is no*

---

[12] Fuller, *Foundations*, pp. 167f., 126f.
[13] Hahn, *Titles*, pp. 372, 399 (italics added).

*evidence that the Church interpreted Jesus as Elijah.*[14]

In the New Testament guild, however, few opinions are held with absolute unanimity. Returning from the view of Fuller and Hahn to Cullmann's *Christology*, for example, one finds a somewhat different picture:

> The synoptic writers did not express their personal faith in Jesus by means of this conception (the Eschatological Prophet). On the other hand, it does seem to have had a certain meaning for the writer of the Fourth Gospel. His particular emphasis of the fact that the Baptist rejected for himself the title of the Prophet, *the returned Elijah*, suggests that the writer of John *wants to reserve this title for Jesus —* along with other Christological designations and concepts, of course.[15]

Cullmann continues by commenting on christological data in the early chapters of Acts, and concludes that within the New Testament only the Gospel of John and the first (Jewish Christian) part of Acts consider Jesus to be the eschatological prophet.[16] To be sure, Cullmann essentially superimposes the figures of the Mosaic prophet and Elijah *redivivus*. Yet just in this way it is clear that we have here an opinion at variance with that of Hahn and Fuller: In the Fourth Gospel and the early chapters of Acts we find literary remains from elements of the post-Easter Church which in fact did view Jesus as—among other things—the eschatological Elijah.[17] And if one desires a yet bolder and clearer

---

[14] The tendency neatly to allot the figure of Elijah to the Baptist and the figure of the Mosaic prophet to Jesus is also reflected in the learned and highly instructive article on Elijah written by J. Jeremias: 'Ηλ(ε)ίας in *TWNT*, ed. G. Kittel, II (Stuttgart, 1935), 930-43.

[15] Cullmann, *Christology*, p. 37 (italics added).

[16] *Ibid.*, p. 38.

[17] I shall adhere to this nomenclature in what follows, for it seems to me that the expression "Elijah *redivivus*," while having the advantage of common use, is quite inappropriate in light of that element which is mainly responsible for the vitality of Elijah traditions: the Tishbite did not die, but was translated to heaven. When he comes, therefore, he is "the eschatological Elijah."

statement, J. A. T. Robinson is obliging:

> According to this very primitive Christology [Acts 3:12-26], Jesus is quite explicitly the Prophet like Moses (as he is also in Stephen's speech in Acts 7:37). It should hardly therefore come as a shock to find that *he is equally evidently Elijah in all but name*. . . . Jesus was indeed to be the Christ. But *he was Elijah first*.[18]

The issue is joined, at least in a preliminary way, and the arena for debate is fixed: the Fourth Gospel and Acts. To attempt a complete resifting of the data would take us, therefore, to both of these documents. But since the arguments of Hahn and Fuller are basically *ex silentio*, the first question is whether *either* document reflects an early Christian identification of Jesus as Elijah. In the compass of the present essay we shall inquire whether such an identification may be reflected in the Fourth Gospel.

## II. ELIJAH IN THE FOUR GOSPELS

Before we turn our attention directly to the Fourth Gospel, it will be well to make a brief survey of the obviously pertinent data in the other Gospels. Synoptic tradition preserves six major and explicit references to Elijah: (1) Opinions among the common folk as to Jesus' identity include—as the second of three possibilities—the suggestion that he is Elijah (Mk. 6:14-16; Lk.

---

[18] J. A. T. Robinson, "Elijah, John and Jesus: An Essay in Detection," *NTS* IV (1958), 277 (the first set of italics added). Cf. W. D. Davies, *The Setting of the Sermon on the Mount* (Cambridge, England, 1964), p. 160, where Davies speaks of Christians who claimed to have had their Elijah and his interpretation of the Law, thus implying, unless I misread him, a Christian group which identified Jesus as Elijah. For a critique of Robinson's provocative article and of Cullmann's views given above, see the tightly argued study by John Knox, "The 'Prophet' in New Testament Christology," in *Lux in Lumine, Essays To Honor W. Norman Pittenger*, ed. R. A. Norris, Jr. (New York, 1966), pp. 23-34. Reasons for my not finding Knox's argument entirely convincing will emerge in the course of the present essay.

9:7-9). (2) When Jesus asks his disciples who he is popularly held to be, they mention the same possibilities, again with Elijah as the second of the three (Mk. 8:27-30; Mt. 16:13-20; Lk. 9:18-21). (3) In the transfiguration Jesus talks with Elijah and Moses (Mk. 9:2-10; Mt. 17:1-9; Lk. 9:28-36). (4) Asked by his disciples why the scribes say it is necessary for Elijah to come first, Jesus affirms the saying and implicitly applies it to the Baptist (Mk. 9:11-13; Mt. 17:10-13; no Lucan parallel). (5) Jesus, speaking to the crowds about the Baptist, explicitly identifies the latter as Elijah (Mt. 11:14; no Lucan parallel). (6) Hearing Jesus' cry from the cross, some of the bystanders opine that he is calling on Elijah, and propose to wait to see whether the Tishbite will come to his aid (Mk. 15:33-36; Mt. 27:45-49; no Lucan parallel).[19]

As regards our present concern the major dimensions of these references can be grasped in two statements: (a) Some of Jesus' contemporaries are represented as holding him to be Elijah (Mark, Matthew, Luke). (b) Jesus himself holds the Baptist to be Elijah (implicitly in Mark, explicitly in Matthew).

When one turns from these Synoptic data to a rereading of the Fourth Gospel, surprises are in store. All six references are absent. Specifically, the possible identification of Jesus as Elijah is nowhere mentioned; nor does Jesus identify the Baptist as Elijah. Instead, the Tishbite emerges explicitly in only one passage, and there in a negative role, so to speak.

### John 1:20f.; 1:25

John 1:18 clearly marks the end of the prologue; 1:51 promises a vision which in fact is then given in the remainder of the Gospel; and the resulting literary piece made up of 1:19-50 divides

---

[19] It is often noted that Luke seems to view Jesus somewhat in terms of Elijah and, correspondingly, that he seems to suppress the linking of Elijah to the Baptist. See, e.g., W. Wink, *John the Baptist in the Gospel Tradition* (London, 1968), pp. 42f. In both regards we see one of the numerous points at which Luke and the fourth evangelist show (or preserve) similar attitudes. On Luke 1:17, see the passage from Wink cited above and R. E. Brown, *The Birth of the Messiah* (New York, 1977), pp. 275ff.

itself into two paragraphs: The Witness of the Baptist (1:19-34), and The First Disciples (1:35-50). It is the first of these paragraphs which contains the only two explicit references to Elijah in the Gospel, 1:20f. and 1:25.

In apparent contradistinction to the Synoptic passages in which the Baptist is identified as Elijah, he is here portrayed as explicitly denying that role for himself. Indeed, he solemnly denies for himself three titles or roles: the Christ, Elijah, the (Mosaic) prophet.

"Who are you?"
And he confessed, and he did not deny, and he confessed,
"I am not the Christ."
And they asked him, "What then?
Are you Elijah?"
And he said, "I am not."
"Are you the prophet?"
And he answered, "No."

Why these solemn denials?

To many interpreters the Baptist's denials have not seemed enormously perplexing. The dominant explanation is close at hand: whether to refute Baptist sectarians known to him or simply to provide dramatic contrast, the evangelist has the Baptist deny that he is the Christ, Elijah, and the (Mosaic) prophet as a prelude to the granting of these titles or roles to Jesus.[20] As re-

---

[20] I express, of course, nothing other than my own opinion when I call this "the dominant explanation." There are at least two other hypotheses which should be mentioned. (1) The Baptist's denial that he is Elijah may be quite simply an accurate historical reminiscence, as Robinson, "Detection," and R. E. Brown are inclined to think. See Brown, *John*, for discussion. This explanation is surely possible, but it seems to me to take too little account of the striking parallelism presented by the three denials and the solemnity with which they are introduced. (2) The evangelist may cause the Baptist to deny that he is Elijah because to allow him that role would imply the Elijah—Christ patterns held by Trypho in Justin's *Dialogue*, notably that the Christ is unaware of his own mission, is dependent on Elijah for his being revealed to men, and is a mere man among men. This is the hypothesis advanced by M. de

gards the first and third this explanation has obvious merits. By tracing the titles "Christ" and "prophet" through the Gospel, one notices that the evangelist does in fact place them in dramatic relief: the Baptist is neither; Jesus is both.[21] The explanation fails, however, with respect to the second. While the Baptist is also made to deny that he is Elijah, the contrasting positive affirmation for Jesus is nowhere forthcoming. Regarding Elijah, the Evangelist is subsequently silent, even at the expense of leaving the Baptist's second denial somewhat dangling.

Returning to our initial question—does the Fourth Gospel contain evidence of an early Christian identification of Jesus as Elijah?—this silence erects a sort of roadblock, not taken with sufficient seriousness, perhaps, by Cullmann and J. A. T. Robinson. Acknowledging the roadblock, one may be led to realize that Hahn and Fuller are correct. At least as regards the Fourth Gospel,

. . . there is no evidence that the post-Easter church ever interpreted Jesus as . . . Elijah *redivivus.* . . .

---

Jonge in a study, one of the virtues of which is that it takes quite seriously the Baptist's second denial ("Jewish Expectations about the 'Messiah' according to the Fourth Gospel," *NTS* 19 [1973], 246-270). De Jonge recognizes the difficulties introduced by citing a text from the mid-second century to illustrate the background of the Fourth Gospel. I myself should not judge those difficulties to be insurmountable whenever there are clear points of contact to link the two texts. It is, however, such clear points of contact that I do not find in de Jonge's presentation. To return to what I have called "the dominant explanation," let me say that for our present purposes it does not greatly matter whether one speaks of the evangelist as refuting Baptist sectarians or as simply providing dramatic contrast, although the Syriac text of the Pseudo-Clementine *Recognitions* I.54 must surely be allowed some weight in support of the former, as R. E. Brown seems somewhat more inclined to do in "Jesus and Elisha," *Perspective* XII (1971), 86, than he is in his commentary. We shall see below that polemic with Baptist sectarians may be at least as clearly reflected in one of the evangelist's sources as in his own work.

[21] See Martyn, *History and Theology*, pp. 110-127, and note the opinion that the evangelist shows a finely nuanced position regarding Jesus' identification with the Mosaic prophet.

Alternatively, however, reading and rereading John 1:20-21 may lead one to be somewhat perseverant. The style of the verses, the careful balancing of the three titles or roles, the steadily decreasing length of the Baptist's answers, and, not least, the solemnity with which he is made to introduce his negative responses—"and he confessed, and he did not deny, and he confessed"—are factors which combine to cause one to assume that the Baptist's three negations are intended to constitute a three-membered instance of parallelism. Thus, one may be driven to try to peer a bit beyond the roadblock. Is there, in fact, no positive role for Elijah after the Baptist's solemn denial of that role for himself?

At this point two paths may be pursued to see whether they lead beyond the impasse. First, one may comb the Gospel for possible Elijah-like traits in the portrait of Jesus. And, second, one may ask whether the absence of an explicitly positive sequel to the Baptist's second negation may be a riddle that has resulted from the evangelist's editing of one of his sources.

## III. ELIJAH-LIKE TRAITS IN THE FOURTH GOSPEL'S PORTRAIT OF JESUS

In order to read through the Fourth Gospel, alert for the possibility of Elijah-like traits in the portrait of Jesus, we must first attempt to summarize the major traditions and expectations attaching to Elijah in second-temple Judaism.

### A. Major Traditions about Elijah

Interpreters commonly remark that no biblical figure so exercised the Jewish imagination of the early centuries B.C.E. and C.E. as did Elijah.[22] While the material is, therefore, un-

---

[22] P. Billerbeck, *Kommentar zum Neuen Testament*, 5 vols. (Munich, 1922-56), IV, 764; Jeremias, *TWNT*, II, 930f.; G. Molin, "Elijahu der Prophet und sein Weiterleben in den Hoffnungen des Judentums und der Christenheit," *Jud* VIII (1952), 65. See also the pertinent

commonly rich, it may not lead to oversimplification to note that three elements in the prophet's Old Testament portrait are chiefly responsible for such remarkable vitality.

## 1. Elijah's Translation

The story of Elijah's translation (2 Kgs. 2:1-12a) is fundamental to all subsequent speculation about him. Since he was dramatically taken up into heaven, he was considered to be alive, in heaven with the (other?) angels,[23] and available, either by being equidistant, so to speak, from every generation, or by being on the verge of coming at the end-time—a fascinating figure indeed.

## 2. Elijah's Miracles

The translated one had been, during his time on earth, the awesome worker of miracles, and the accounts of those mighty deeds were told and retold. Josephus, for example, repeats the stories of 1 Kings 17, Elijah's miraculous provision of meal and oil to the poor widow of Zarephath, and his restoration of her son to life (*Ant.* VIII; XIII.2-3; supplemented from Menander). Moreover, not only were the stories of the earthly Elijah repeated, but also their major accents were combined with the portrait of the translated one, producing the rich image of an Elijah who could fly down to earth in order miraculously to aid those in deep distress (cf. Mark 15:35f.). Numerous legends developed from this combination.[24]

---

sections in *Élie le Prophète*, Gustave Bardy *et al.*, eds., 2 vols. (Burges, 1956), notably M. J. Stiassny, "Le Prophète Élie dans le Judaïsme," II, 199-255, and M. E. Boismard, "Élie dans le Nouveau Testament," I, 116-28.

[23] The precise location of Elijah, given as heaven in 2 Kgs. 2:11 and in 1 *Enoch* 89:52, was a subject of some debate among the rabbis (Billerbeck, IV, 765f.).

[24] L. Ginzberg, *The Legends of the Jews*, 7 vols. (Philadelphia, 1910-39), IV, 202ff.; cf. also M. Segal, *Elijah, A Study in Jewish Folklore* (New York, 1935), *passim*.

## 3. Elijah's Expected Coming

Precisely at the beginning of the second-temple period, "Malachi" announced that God would send a messenger before his own final advent (Mal. 3:1); and a later hand, in all probability, identified this messenger, understandably enough, with the translated Elijah who was therefore expected to come (3:1) in order to restore the hearts of fathers to their children, and the hearts of children to their fathers (3:23f.), thus mitigating God's wrath. To this portrait Ben Sira (48:10) added an element drawn from the "Servant of Yahweh" traditions (Is. 49:6), thus viewing the coming Elijah as the one who will restore the tribes of Israel. And beyond Ben Sira numerous traditions developed, the major motif being that in preparation for God's eschatological advent—and hence as the "messianic" figure himself—Elijah would come to accomplish, often miraculously, the *restitutio in integrum* of God's people. In the traditions about his eschatological coming, Elijah is expected to do many things, such as make peace, whether within families or in the whole world; reassemble the members of the people who have been taken away; determine which are the genuine Israelites, thus re-establishing the purity of corpus Israel; restore to Israel the manna, the sprinkling water, and the anointing oil; raise the dead, thus vanquishing death as he once vanquished the prophets of Baal.[25]

---

[25] In addition to the works cited in nn. 22 and 24, see E. Schürer, *A History of the Jewish People in the Time of Christ*, 6 vols. (Edinburgh, 1890-91), index; G. H. Dalman, *Jesus-Jeshua: Studies in the Gospels* (New York, 1929), pp. 124f., 164f., 205f.; and G. F. Moore, *Judaism in the First Centuries of the Christian Era*, 3 vols. (Cambridge, 1927-30), II, 357ff. Representative references may be listed as follows: *make peace*—Mal. 3:24 (familial peace); Sir. 48:10 (restoring order to the nation); Mt. 17:11 and Mk. 9:12 (cosmic order); *Ed.* 8:7 (world peace) *Reassemble the tribe*—Sir. 48:10; *Ed.* 8:7. *Purify corpus Israel*—*Ed.* 8:7 shows debate on this subject; in any case some rabbis held that Elijah would determine whom to reject and whom to admit as true Israelites (cf. Jn. 1:47). *Restore manna*, etc.—*Mek. Exod.* 16:33. *Raise the dead*—Sota 9:15; *pShab.* I. 3c, 7 and I. 3c, 20; cf. Billerbeck, *Kommentar*, I, 194; Jeremias (*TWNT*, II, 934, n. 45) comments that Elijah's raising the dead is found in late texts, but see Schürer, *History*, II, 2, 157; Ginzberg, *Legends*, IV, 227f., 243, 246, n. 21, and compare the comments to Luke

In short, the first two major elements—the translation to heaven and the miracles—find their home by flowing into the third—the expected coming—producing the image of the eschatological Elijah as a miraculous helper who comes to restore the people of Israel just prior to God's own advent.[26]

---

7:1ff. by H. Schürmann, *Das Lukasevangelium,* Erster Teil (Fribourg, 1969), pp. 398ff. I see no good reason to doubt that the expectation of Elijah's raising the dead was alive in the first century, precisely in connection with 1 Kings 17:17ff. To the five activities of the eschatological Elijah I have listed, others could, of course, be added. See particularly Ginzberg, *Legends,* IV, 233ff. New Testament students will sense the absence from my list of a reference to the calling of Israel to "repentance," as distinct from "restoring" Israel (Mal. 3:23f.). I have omitted this item because, while it may be implied in Malachi 3:23f., and while it is explicitly mentioned in *Pirke R. Eliezer* 43, I am not at all certain that the firm and focused connection between Elijah and the call to repentance as such was made without John the Baptist serving as the middle term (cf. Ginzberg, *Legends,* IV, 233). Talmudic students, on the other hand, will note that I have not mentioned Elijah's role in clarifying obscure points of Torah. Cf. the comment of Davies, *Sermon on the Mount,* p. 160, and *Ed.* 8:7 (arrange disputes) and *B.M.* 1:8; 2.8; 3,4,5; *Shek.* 2.5. This function of Elijah would seem to belong closely to that of making peace.

[26] In light of the strong tendency to connect the eschatological Elijah with John the Baptist (and not with Jesus), it may be pertinent to mention three regards in which the Baptist would seem to fit rather poorly the dominant Elijah motifs (*pace* Jeremias: "The NT Understanding of Elijah Expectation: Fulfilled in John the Baptist," *TWNT,* II, 938): (a) The eschatological Elijah is concerned to restore the purity of corpus Israel before God's coming, holding precisely, as Jeremias says, that "blood purity alone entitles one to a share in end-time salvation" (936); the Baptist, by contrast, preaches a radical repentance, holding that blood descendancy is irrelevant to the question of salvation (Mt. 4:9f.; Lk. 3:8f.). (b) What we might call the "classic" portrait of the eschatological Elijah shows him as the forerunner not of the Messiah, as the Baptist is portrayed, but rather of God. To be sure it is obvious that in some Jewish sources Elijah came to be viewed as the forerunner of the Messiah, but one is at least entitled to wonder whether this development may not be paradoxically indebted somehow to an early Christian syllogism: Jesus is the Messiah; the Baptist was Elijah; Elijah is therefore the forerunner of the Messiah. And if that should be the case, we have a second point of discontinuity between the Elijah expectations and the Baptist. (The earliest firmly datable texts showing Elijah as the forerunner of *the Messiah* present two virtually identical comments made in

## B. Elijah-Like Traits in the Fourth Gospel's Portrait of Jesus?

In the compass of a relatively brief essay there is not adequate space to explore all possibilities attaching to this question, nor is that necessary. Bearing in mind the major accents in the sketch given above, it will suffice to inquire whether they are reflected in the portrait of Jesus.

### 1. Elijah's Translation

We must begin on a negative note, for there is good reason to read John 3:13 as a polemic, not only against the possible identification of Jesus as Elijah, but also against the view that Elijah was translated at all: "No one has ascended into heaven but he who has descended from heaven, the Son of Man."[27] To be sure, Wayne Meeks has made a strong case that the polemic is directed against claims for Moses,[28] but Elijah traditions are probably also in the picture. Indeed Meeks himself refers in a note to H. Odeberg's view that behind the Fourth Gospel stood a polemic

---

Justin's *Dialogue* by the Jew Trypho [8:4 and 49:1], but a non-Christian Jewish origin for the pattern can scarcely be affirmed on such a slim basis. I am content to cite R. E. Brown, adding italics at only one point: "The rabbinic evidence for making Elijah the forerunner of the Messiah is later than the time of Jesus, but passages like Mark 9:11 *suggest* that this idea was current in the first century" [*Perspective* XII, 100]. It seems to be one of those matters on which certainty is not in our grasp.) (c) Recalling how pervasive in those expectations is the role of the Tishbite as miraculous helper, one must consider the absence of such a note in the Synoptic portraits of the Baptist as one who is not at all a miracle worker. (The thrust of John 10:41, especially of the clause, "John [the Baptist] did no sign," is something of a puzzle. In addition to the commentaries see E. Bammel, " 'John Did No Miracle'; John 10:41," in *Miracles*, ed. C. F. D. Moule (London, 1965), pp. 179-202, and W. Wink, *John the Baptist*, pp. 97f. The thesis to which the present study leads would suggest that this negative clause is purposely harmonious with the Baptist's negation of the role of Elijah for himself. That role and its miracles attach solely to Jesus.)

[27] The additional clause "he who is in heaven" is almost certainly secondary. See the commentaries.

[28] Meeks, *Prophet-King*, p. 301.

against "the traditions of ascensions into heaven by great saints, patriarchs, and prophets of old . . . such as Enoch, Abraham, Moses, Elijah, Isaiah. . . ."[29] And Odeberg, following Billerbeck, had cited a pertinent saying attributed to Rabbi Yose ben Halafta (ca. 150 C.E.) in which the ascensions of Moses and Elijah are alike denied:

> Never did Shekina descend on earth, nor did Moses and Elijah ascend on high. . . . How can it be maintained that Moses and Elijah did not ascend to heaven? And, lo, it is written (Exod. 19:3): "And Moses went up unto God." There was a distance of ten fingers' breadth. But, lo, it is written (II Kgs. 2:11): "And Elijah went up by a whirlwind into heaven". Even here it is to be understood that there was a distance of three fingers' breadth.[30]

Doubtless the motivation for the polemic of Rabbi ben Halafta will have been different from that which may lie behind the formulation of John 3:13. The point is simply that the rabbinic passage would seem to strengthen the possibility that the evangelist wishes to suppress the portraits of both Moses and Elijah as ones who ascended to heaven. *Only Jesus* is the ascended one, and, as regards our present concern, precisely not as Elijah, but rather as the Son of Man.

This first datum lends support to the views of Hahn and Fuller, and seems to run precisely counter to the statement by Cullmann that "the writer of John wants to reserve this title [Elijah] for Jesus."

## 2. Elijah's Miracles

Here we encounter data which point rather clearly in the other direction. We begin with two of John's miracle stories which

---

[29] *Ibid.*, p. 301 note, quoting from H. Odeberg, *The Fourth Gospel* (Uppsala, 1929), p. 97.

[30] *Suk. 5a*, following Odeberg's text, *Fourth Gospel*, pp. 89f.; note also *Mek.* on Exod. 19:10, cited by Meeks, *Prophet-King*, p. 205.

seem quite immediately to show just the sort of traits we might expect of the miracle-working, eschatological Elijah.

### (a) The Changing of Water into Wine (2:1-11)

Commenting on this passage, R. E. Brown mentions Elijah's miraculous furnishing of meal and oil to the widow of Zarephath in 1 Kings 17:1-16. R. T. Fortna, following A. Schulz, suggests the possibility that 2:5 may show a parallel "to the claim Elijah and Elisha make on those at hand to assist in a miracle." G. Reim suggests that John 2:4a may be an allusion to 1 Kings 17:18 (but see also Gen. 41:55).[31] It would indeed seem pertinent to remark that many Jews and/or Jewish Christians of the first century would think above all of Elijah when hearing a story of a miracle which answers "an unexpected physical need that in the particular circumstances cannot be satisifed by natural means."[32] The changing of water into wine may thus paint a picture of Jesus which includes accents reminiscent of Elijah's first deed of mercy to the widow. It is numbered as the first of Jesus' signs (2:11).

### (b) The Healing of the Nobleman's Son (4:46-54)

This is numbered as the second of Jesus' signs (4:54), and it may reflect in part the second of Elijah's miracles for the widow of Zarephath, the restoring of her son to life. In John 4:50 Jesus says to the nobleman, "Go, your son lives," a sentence which Reim classifies as an "obvious allusion" to Elijah's remark to the widow (1 Kgs. 17:23), "Look, your son lives."[33] We may also note

---

[31]R. E. Brown, *John,* I, 101; R. T. Fortna, *The Gospel of Signs* (London, 1970), p. 32 (see also the note on that page referring to A. Schulz, who mentions the possible parallels of 2:6 to 1 Kings 18:34 and of 2:8 to 2 Kings 4:41); G. Reim, *Studien zum alttestamentlichen Hintergrund des Johannesevangeliums* (Cambridge, 1974), p. 157. That Reim speaks of a "probable allusion" to 1 Kings 17:18 in John 2:4 may somewhat overstate the case, since the Hebraic idiom "What to me and to you?" is not infrequently encountered in the Old Testament. Above all, I do not mean to suggest that the story in 1 Kings 17 is the sole element in the background of John 2:1-11, even if I cannot say that I find the recent argument of E. Linnemann to be convincing ("Die Hochzeit zu Kana und Dionysos," *NTS* XX [1973-74], 408-418). Note especially Paul W. Meyer, "John 2:10," *JBL* LXXXVI (1967), 191-197.

[32]Brown, *John*, I, 101.

[33]Reim, *Studien*, p. 156; cf. Fortna, *Signs*, p. 42.

that the second sign is closely patterned on the first.[34] In the picture of Jesus presented by these first two signs, therefore, a Jewish reader steeped in the Elijah stories would probably sense at some level of consciousness certain traits reminiscent of the great helper; and, if we bring into our purview also material from the Elisha cycle, bearing in mind the close connection between the two figures in some patterns of Jewish thinking,[35] the number of pertinent data increases.

### (c) The Feeding of the Multitude (6:1-14)

While there can be no doubt that Moses traditions lie directly in the background of this story, there are also several striking parallels with the story of Elisha's miraculous provision of bread in 2 Kings 4:42-44.[36]

| 2 Kings | John |
|---|---|
| 4:42  A man came . . . bringing twenty loaves of barley | 6:9  There is a lad here who has five barley loaves[37] |

---

[34]Brown, *John*, I, 194.

[35]I am inclined to think that R. E. Brown has rightly warned us against an easy confusing of "the resemblances between Jesus and Elijah with the resemblances between Jesus and Elisha," in his perceptive and provocative article, *Perspective* XII, 85-104, citation from p. 85. We should begin our research by considering the two prophets separately, not least because one was translated, whereas the other died. Yet we may also allow for a degree of coalescence in light of the extremely close connection between the two, signaled by Elisha's receiving a double portion of Elijah's spirit (cf. Luke 1:17). One notes numerous points of overlapping between the two figures in Jewish tradition (Ginzberg, *Legends*, IV, 239ff.).

[36]Reim, *Studien*, p. 157.

[37]The Synoptics have only "loaves" and thus provide in this regard a less precise parallel to the Elisha story. Indeed, remarking that the two terms "made of barley" and "young child" occur only here in the NT, Fortna (*Signs*, pp. 58f.), following C. K. Barrett (*The Gospel According to St. John* [London, 1955], p. 229), also notes the presence of the latter in the story immediately preceding the one in 2 Kings 4:42ff.

| 4:43a | . . . his servant said, "How am I to set this before a hundred men?" | 6:9 | . . . but, what are they among so many? |
|---|---|---|---|
| 4:43b -44 | So he repeated, "Give them to the men, that they may eat, for thus says the Lord, 'They shall eat and have some left'." So he set it before them. And they ate and had some left. . . . | 6:13 | So they gathered them up and filled twelve baskets with fragments from the five barley loaves, left by those who had eaten. |

*(d) The Healing of the Man Born Blind (9:1-7)*

The comparison here is, of course, with Elisha's healing of Naaman.[38]

|  | *2 Kings* |  | *John* |
|---|---|---|---|
| 5:10 | Go and wash in the Jordan seven times. | 9:7a | Go, wash in the pool of Siloam. . . .[39] |
| 5:14 | So he went down and dipped himself seven times in the Jordan . . . and his flesh was restored. . . . | 9:7b | So he went and washed and came back seeing. |

Doubtless other "allusions" and "parallels" could be mentioned with various degrees of probability. I shall mention only the one which arises most clearly from the argument of Reim about John 11:41f., and which brings us back to the Elijah cycle.

*(e) The Raising of Lazarus (11:1-44)*

At the crucial point in the highly dramatic account, Jesus relates the Father to himself and to the bystanders by means of a prayer:

Father, I thank thee that thou hast heard me. I know that

---

[38] Reim, *Studien*, pp. 157ff.

[39] Fortna's comment about "the claim Elijah and Elisha make on those at hand to assist in a miracle" (*Signs*, p. 32), is referred by him to John 6:10, 12; 9:7; 11:39; and 21:6.

thou hearest me always, but I have said this on account of the people standing by, that they may believe that thou didst send me (11:41f.).

Reim suggests a comparison with the story of Elijah's contest with the Baal prophets on Mount Carmel.[40] At the crucial point in that dramatic story Elijah prays similarly:

O Lord God of Abraham, Isaac, and Israel, let it be known this day that thou art God in Israel and that I am thy servant. . . . Hear me, O Lord, hear me, that this people may know that thou art the Lord God (1 Kgs. 18:36f.).[41]

The case for linking John 11:41f. to 1 Kings 18:37 is surely not so strong as those we have presented in the earlier instances. Reim seems clearly to recognize this, for he lists five points in support of this link, saying that he does so against possible skepticism.[42] Were this suggested link standing alone, one would scarcely speak, I think, of a "probable allusion." Yet, in light of the others, I should be inclined to grant that it is at least clearly possible. In any case, the noting of striking allusions in four of the miracle stories and the possibility of one in a fifth story will suffice to suggest that the miracle-working figures of Elijah and, secondarily, Elisha have indeed provided some of the features of the Gospel's miracle-working Jesus.

## 3. Elijah's Expected Coming

Since it is clear throughout the Gospel—note, for example 1:35-51—that Jesus is *the* eschatological figure, all of the data we

---

[40] Reim, *Studien*, p. 157.

[41] Note also *Ber. 9b* (cited by Ginzberg, *Legends*, IV, 199), interpreting Elijah's double exclamation (Hear me, hear me!): "He spoke: Lord of the world, thou wilt send me as a messenger at the end time, but if my words do not meet with fulfillment now, the Jews cannot be expected to believe me in the latter days," and compare with the motif of the sent messenger in John 11:41f.

[42] Reim, *Studien*, p. 219.

have just surveyed under the second category are also pertinent here. Indeed, we may consider it to be at least possible that the Elijah- (and Elisha-) like traits lie in the five miracle stories because the author(s) of these stories believed the eschatological Elijah had come in Jesus. Moreover there is the striking confession which climaxes the story of the miraculous feeding:

> When the people saw the sign which he had done, they said, "This is indeed the prophet who is to come into the world" (6:14).

I have already noted that the feeding story reflects imprints from at least two traditions: the miraculous provision of bread by Elisha and the expectation of eschatological manna at the hands of the Mosaic prophet. There may also be an indication that Elijah plays a role in this climactic verse. One observes that the term "the prophet" (the Mosaic prophet) is provided with the appositional expression "who is to come, etc." Now the Mosaic prophet is regularly said to be "raised up" by God (cf. the fountain text of Deut. 18:15; also Acts 3:22, 26; 7:37),[43] rather than to be one who "comes."[44] On the other hand, "the coming one" may be some-

---

[43] The import of the verb "to arise" is one of the factors supporting the reading of p[66] and p[75] in John 7:52. One hopes that future editions of the very helpful and widely used *The Greek New Testament*, ed. Aland *et al.*, 2d ed. (New York, 1969) will at least cite this reading, and, even better, select it.

[44] There are, to be sure, a few texts which link Moses with the verb "to come," notably in the Samaritan sources; see Meeks, *Prophet-King*, pp. 246ff. Compare also the Fragmentary Targum of Palestine on Exodus 12:42, cited by *ibid.*, pp. 213f. The NT evidence, on the other hand, seems clearly to reflect a pattern: leaving John 6:14 aside, in all instances in which explicit identifications of the Mosaic prophet and of the eschatological Elijah are linked with one of our verbs, the former is said *to be raised up*, while the latter is said *to come*. For the eschatological Elijah see the data presented at the beginning of Section II above, and for the Mosaic prophet see Acts 3:22 (cf. 3:26); Acts 7:37; John 7:52; perhaps Luke 7:16. See also the preceding note.

thing close to a technical term for the eschatological Elijah.[45] Thus John 6:14 may provide a climax for the feeding story by referring to Jesus both as the Mosaic prophet and as the eschatological Elijah. And if that is the case, we may think of John 6:1-14 not only in connection with Elisha, but also in connection with Elijah himself. Indeed this text may show that—however distinct from one another the figures of John 1:20f. may be— when it comes to the *portrait* of Jesus, the miracle stories are penned in such a way as to allow an easy coalescence among the figures of Moses, Elijah, and Elisha.

---

[45] R. E. Brown, *John* I, 44; a more detailed argument in Brown, "Three Quotations from John the Baptist in the Gospel of John," *CBQ* XXII (1960), 292-298 (esp. 297): "[1] Mal. 3, 1 has the words: 'Behold he is coming,' seemingly applied to the messenger sent to prepare the way. [2] When in Mt. 11, 3-14 the disciples of John the Baptist ask Jesus if he is the one *who is to come* (*erchomenos*), he answers that John the Baptist is 'Elias, *who is to come* (*mellon erchesthai*)'. [3] And the characteristics John the Baptist attributes to the one who is to come are amazingly Elias-like." One will want to note, on the other hand, the opinion of Meeks, *Prophet-King*, p. 90: "It is often supposed that 'the coming one' was a messianic title, but this cannot be demonstrated." See also a similar position in Hahn, *Titles*, p. 393. I am inclined to feel that, while the general arguments against which Hahn and Meeks were reacting may be subject to objections, a specific link between numerous occurrences of the participial expression and some of the hopes for the eschatological Elijah enjoys some degree of probability. Note particularly Hahn, *Titles*, p. 380. In a forthcoming study I shall explore this matter in connection with the expressions in John 1:15, 27, 30. Meanwhile one may be permitted at least to wonder whether the texts linking Moses with the verb "to come" (see preceding note) may not have arisen at least in part because Elijah-like traits were transferred to the Mosaic prophet. (To be sure, one would strongly doubt this in connection with the Samaritan evidence, since the Samaritans recognized only the Pentateuch.) Perhaps the bold hypothesis of O. Bauernfeind regarding an Elijah/Moses source, which he supposed to lie behind part of Peter's speech in Acts 3, is, *qua* literary hypothesis, as wide of the mark as E. Haenchen believes (*The Acts of the Apostles* [Philadelphia, 1971], pp. 210f.); yet the *religionsgeschichtliche* dimensions of the hypothesis may have some value. Of course, it is a coalescing of the figures of Moses and Elijah which I am suggesting for the combined expressions in John 6:14. It may be the case, nevertheless, that the author of the verse was to some degree aware of the coalescence, especially in light of John 1:20f.

## C. Conclusion

Reading through the Fourth Gospel while seeking to be alert
for Elijah-like traits in the portrait of Jesus has not brought to our
attention data which one would classify as conclusive "evidence
that the post-Easter Church ever interpreted Jesus as . . . Elijah
*redivivus*." We have found, rather, a divided picture. On the one
side stands 3:13, which seems to say that Jesus, as the Son of Man
and emphatically not as Elijah, is the only one ever to ascend to
heaven. On the other side are 2:1ff., 4:43ff., 6:1ff., 11:41f. (also
9:1ff. by the inclusion of Elisha traditions), which seem clearly to
bring Elijah-like traits into the portrait of Jesus. How is this divided picture to be explained?

When one observes that the negative datum lies in a Son of
Man saying very probably formulated by the evangelist—note
the descending-ascending pattern—whereas the positive data
consistently emerge in the miracle-story tradition, a two-part
hypothesis lies close at hand:

1. Perhaps the three denials placed in the Baptist's mouth
(1:20f.) stem from a pre-Johannine author who also collected and
shaped the miracle stories—or at least five of them—in such a
way as to provide positive counterparts to all three denials.
Should one be convinced of this much, he *might* conclude that he
is faced with evidence of at least one theologian of the post-Easter
Church who, without being explicit about it, did in fact interpret
Jesus as Elijah.

2. It would follow that the evangelist, while satisfied to allow
*minor* Elijah-like *traits* to remain in some of the miracle stories,
penned 3:13 in such a way as emphatically to exclude, among
other things, an explicit identification of Jesus as the eschatological Elijah. And if this last suggestion should recommend itself as a
good possibility, one may be led to inquire whether the evangelist
may not have suppressed in the materials inherited from the predecessor precisely what has thus far been missing: a direct counterpart to the Baptist's second denial, an explicit identification of
Jesus as Elijah.

## IV. A DIVIDED PICTURE AND SOURCE CRITICISM

We begin with an observation which in and of itself may go quite some way toward testing the initial part of this hypothesis. There is the simple fact that the Baptist's three denials and all of the data which we have discovered to show Elijah- (and Elisha-) like traits in Jesus' portrait fall in sections of the Gospel assigned by a number of critics to a pre-Johannine source.[46] To be sure, it would be unwise confidently to build extensive theories on the basis of the present state of Johannine source criticism. One needs only to mention the commentaries of R. E. Brown and Barnabas Lindars to be reminded that some leading interpreters find the labors of Johannine source critics largely unconvincing.[47] For three reasons, however, I believe that a considerable degree of confidence is warranted in the present instance.

1. The question before us involves a modest portion of the source theories—only that there was a signs source which included the Baptist's pointed denials—and, as we shall shortly see, an account of the coming of Jesus' first disciples, in addition to the traditional materials in at least five of the miracle stories. Over this much ground there is extensive, though of course not unanimous, agreement.

2. This extensive agreement has emerged in the careful work

---

[46] I shall take up the work of these critics in a moment. Here one should note some of the recent assessments of the state of source criticism in John's Gospel: D. M. Smith, "The Sources of the Gospel of John: An Assessment of the Present State of the Problem," *NTS* X (1963-64), 336-351; Barnabas Lindars, *Behind the Fourth Gospel* (London, 1971), pp. 27-42 and *passim*; R. Kysar, "The Source Analysis of the Fourth Gospel, A Growing Consensus?" *Nov.T.* XV (1973), 134-152; D. M. Smith, "Johannine Christianity: Some Reflections on Its Character and Delineation," *NTS* XXI (1974-75), 223-248, especially 229; W. A. Meeks, "'Am I a Jew?'—Johannine Christianity and Judaism." in *Christianity, Judaism and Other Greco-Roman Cults,* ed. J. Neusner (Leiden, 1975), I. 163-186. Of the four scholars mentioned here, Smith and Kysar are cautiously optimistic Lindars and Meeks rather pessimistic. One should not overlook Kysar's observations as regards the degree of consensus emerging from a variety of methods.

[47] See particularly the sharp criticism given by Lindars in his lucid booklet, *Behind the Fourth Gospel.*

of four scholars, R. Fortna, J. Becker, W. Nicol, and G. Reim, three of whom (delete Nicol) carried out their labors independently of one another.[48] It would be pertinent to remark, of course, that all of these critics have drawn on Bultmann's analysis of a signs source, but it is equally pertinent to note (a) that Fortna, in particular, worked through the materials with a degree of care and methodological thoroughness not evident in any of the previous attempts, and (b) that, independently of one another, three of the analysts have disagreed with Bultmann in respect to a matter crucial for our present concerns: they all assign to the source not only the core of each of the miracle stories which show the Elijah/Elisha traits, but also the traditional materials in the paragraph containing the Baptist's pointed denials.[49] Such independent agreement must be granted considerable weight.

3. Moreover, there is the fact—not altogether surprising— that the source-critics' labors are specifically related to our questions about the eschatological Elijah. Writing several years ago, Fortna remarked that in the source

---

[48]R. T. Fortna, *Signs*; J. Becker, "Wunder und Christologie," *NTS* XVI (1969-70), 130-148; W. Nicol, *The Sēmeia in the Fourth Gospel*, in *NovT* Sup., no. 32 (Leiden, 1972); Reim, *Studien*. The independence is quite clear in the cases of Fortna and Becker (both 1970), and I am assuming it also for the basic work done by Reim, since that work was a 1967 dissertation (Oxford). My frequent citation of Reim should not be taken to indicate complete agreement. I am afraid I must share some of the reservations noted by R. E. Brown in his review of Reim, *Theol. Studies* XXXV (1974), 558-61. One should also mention the source-critical labors of E. Bammel, *Miracles*, pp. 179-202 (reconstruction of a source he calls *Z* is given on pp. 193ff.), and in his "The Baptist in Early Christian Tradition," *NTS* XVIII (1971-72), 95-128 (esp. 109-113, 122-26). Also D. M. Smith, "The Milleu of the Johannine Miracle Source: A Proposal," R. Hamerton—Kelly and R. Scroggs (eds.) *Jews, Greeks and Christians* (Leiden, 1976), 164-180.

[49]I refer to Fortna, *Signs*, pp. 167ff., Becker *NTS* XVI, 135; and Reim, *Studien*, pp. 208f. Nicol speaks at one point (*Sēmeia*, p. 89) as though he intends to include 1:19ff. in the source, but the statements there are somewhat ambiguous, and his remarks at another juncture (pp. 39f.) even point the other way. His one explicit reference to 1:19ff. follows a statement about the source *and* the rest of John, and is therefore

. . . the parallel is strongest to the Elijah/Elisha tradition. Nowhere is Jesus explicitly identified with either of those earlier prophets, but that the identification is intended is evident in several ways: the Baptist's denial that he is Elijah, implying that Jesus in fact is; the phrase 'of whom the prophets wrote', which probably has at least Mal. 4:5 in mind; and the parallels in the source both to the diction of 1 and 2 Kings (John 4:50, 6:9, 9:7) and to the particular miracles done by Elijah and Elisha (esp. John 6 and 11).[50]

These remarks of Fortna are now made even stronger by a striking and, as I have already noted, independent confirmation in the most recently published portrait of the source, that by Reim. Particularly striking is the fact that Reim's portrait has emerged, not from a study which began as a source-critical attempt, but rather from a probing of the Gospel's Old Testament background. From this point on the compass Reim noticed, among other things,

. . . that in the Gospel of John no allusions to 1 and 2 Kings are found outside of five passages which all stand within the signs-source postulated by various scholars.

And he did not hesitate to draw a conclusion:

We see, then, that the author who assembled the signs-source had a definite interest in presenting the miracle stories of Jesus against the background of the Elijah and Elisha miracles. . . . This little book of miracles was designed to show that one cannot view the Baptist as Elijah or the Prophet— the Baptist himself refuses these roles—but rather only the wonder-working Jesus.[51]

---

of no use as regards the distinction (p. 87).

[50] Fortna, *Signs*, p. 232.

[51] Reim, *Studien*, pp. 207f. Cf. similar remarks on the part of Nicol, *Sēmeia*, p. 89.

In the analyses of these source-critics, one finds, then, confirmation of the first part of our hypothesis: the Baptist's denial that he is Elijah, and the Elijah/Elisha-like traits as applied to Jesus would seem indeed to stand in the text of John because the evangelist inherited them from a predecessor. Contrary to Hahn and Fuller, we have apparently encountered data indicating that at least one early Christian theologian—yet not John himself, as affirmed by Cullmann—did in fact view Jesus as the eschatological Elijah.

Yet some degree of doubt may remain, not only because the source-critical analyses fail to be universally convincing, but also because, as Fortna put it, "Nowhere [in the source] is Jesus explicitly identified with [Elijah]."[52] If the author of the source actually intended to grant to Jesus all three of the "titles" denied for himself by the Baptist, why did he fail to make this intention explicit only in the case of the second? To return to Hahn and Fuller, we may recall that they clearly acknowledge the application to Jesus of "certain traits from the Elijah tradition," and of "a whole series of traits [which] remind us of Elias." Yet they are equally clear with regard to the absence of even one datum showing an explicit interpretation of Jesus as Elijah, and it is precisely the absence of such a datum—the Baptist's second denial is still dangling—which faces us at the end of the path we have followed.

Have we, however, really come to the end of the path? Hardly. There is still that strikingly divided picture presented by the Gospel as it stands, a picture which would seem to be there because of a marked difference in attitude toward an Elijah-like Jesus on the part of the source's author and on the part of the evangelist. *Ex hypothesi* the evangelist is not concerned to expunge minor Elijah-like traits in the miracle stories, but he is determined to exclude as possibly pertinent to the portrait of Jesus that element in the picture of Elijah without which the latter has, so to speak, no vitality—the prophet's ascension to heaven. Now, given both the absence of an explicit identification of Jesus as Elijah and the nature of this divided picture, the question must

---

[52] Fortna, *Signs*, p. 232.

be raised whether the attitude of the source's author was so positive as to cause him to make an explicit identification of Jesus as
Elijah, and, correspondingly, whether the attitude of the evangelist
was so negative as to embolden him to suppress such an explicit
identification.

We should have to admit that it is not possible to go beyond
the mere posing of these questions, were it not the case that
shortly after the Baptist's dangling denial of his being Elijah—en
route, so to speak, from that denial to the miracle stories whose
portrait of Jesus borrows several colors from the pictures of
Elijah—we encounter a verse replete with problems which, in
turn, may indicate both the original Elijah identification by the
author of the source and its suppression at the hands of the
evangelist. The verse stands, one hastens to add, in a paragraph
beginning at John 1:35, the traditional materials of which are assigned to the source by all four source-critics mentioned above.

John 1:43 has drawn a considerable amount of comment from
interpreters precisely because of its vexing problems.[53] There is,
first, the difficulty of identifying the subject of the verb "he
wished to go." Three possibilities are regularly mentioned: One
may take as subject the last person named, Peter; or one may
elect the person who is the subject of the last finite verb, Jesus;
or, taking one's cue from an adverbial reading of "first" in verse
41, one may identify the subject as Andrew, who on this reading
found, first of all, his brother (v. 41), and then, secondly, Philip
(v. 43). As the text stands, there is little doubt that the first and
third of these possibilities are to be excluded. As R. E. Brown
comments, ". . . while John might tell us that Peter found Philip,
he would scarcely stop to tell us that Peter wanted to go to
Galilee."[54] By the same token, as the text now stands, Andrew is
to be excluded; and this leaves the subject as Jesus. It is surely

---

[53] At this point it may be pertinent for me to remark to the reader that
the present study had its origin, not in a critical assessment of the statements by Hahn and Fuller, but rather in several attempts over a period of
time to come to terms with the problems of this single verse. The reader
will find most of the problems clearly defined in Bultmann, *Das
Evangelium des Johannes* (Göttingen, 1950).

[54] R. E. Brown, *John*, I, 81.

Jesus who desires to make the journey, and it is thus Jesus who finds Philip. To make this grammatical decision is not, however, to get rid of the problem. Would an author composing his narrative in a simple and straightforward manner express himself so clumsily?

In the second place, one notes the location of the expressed subject, Jesus. To be sure, verse 43 stands in a passage replete not only with parataxis, but also with the well-known and largely Semitic pattern of placing the verb before the subject. Hence the expression "and said Jesus to him" calls for no special comment. What is striking is the supplying of the subject after the *third* of three verbs, all of which share this same subject.[55] Elsewhere in the paragraph when there is a series of such coordinated verbs, the subject is consistently supplied after the first of them (vv. 41, 45, 47), and this seems generally to be expected in such constructions.[56] To express the problem in less technical language: Would an author, composing freely, employ a finite verb to speak of an impending journey, use a second finite verb to indicate an act of finding, and, finally, use a third verb of speaking, only then providing the subject of all three verbs?

Third, there is the rather abrupt travel notice. Commentators regularly remark that it looks forward to the Cana story, but almost as regularly they express some puzzlement over its being given here.[57] Why does it not come immediately before 2:1?

---

[55] I read verse 43 as three independent clauses of a single sentence, the second and third being introduced by "and." See the note on punctuation in Aland, *Greek New Testament*. I am inclined to think that it is precisely the awkwardness of the text which has caused the majority of modern editors to place a full stop after either the first or the second clause. While that may be sound practice for a modern translator, the exegete is obliged, of course, to deal with the awkwardness.

[56] I have found in the standard handbooks no example of the subject being supplied after the third of three coordinate, finite verbs; nor have consultations with Semitic scholars produced any such instances.

[57] As Bultmann remarks, the travel notice of verse 43 makes it difficult to picture the events which follow (*Johannes*, p. 68). Interpreters also note that the dangling "first" of verse 41 and the form of Philip's claim in verse 45: "we have found," should quite possibly be reckoned as two further problems which arise from the present wording of verse 43.

Finally, and perhaps most tellingly, not a few interpreters have sensed that verse 43 breaks the chain-like character of the gathering of disciples. The remarks of M. E. Boismard are particularly cogent. Having noted that 1:6-8 and 1:9ff. emphasize the primal character of the Baptist's witness, Boismard continues:

> The first link of the chain is given in 1:35-39: two disciples of the Baptist hear him affirm that Jesus is the Messiah, and, on the basis of his word alone, they begin to follow Jesus. Both then believe in Jesus on account of the testimony of the Baptist. . . .

> The second link is given in 1:40-42: Andrew, one of the two disciples, leads his brother Simon to Jesus by declaring to him: "We have found the Christ." Through the agency of Andrew, the faith of Simon clearly links up with the testimony of the Baptist.

> The chain seems to break in 1:43ff. A new person appears, Philip, who is called directly by Christ: "Follow me!" Moreover, it is Philip, and not Andrew, who leads Nathanael to Christ (1:45-47). Neither the faith of Philip nor that of Nathanael is linked to the testimony of the Baptist, then; and that is why the chain seems broken.[58]

A partial solution proposed by Boismard is to identify the second disciple of verses 35-39 as Philip, thus achieving a balanced picture: Andrew and Philip, disciples of the Baptist, first attend to his witness, and then become themselves apostles, both to the Jewish world (to Simon, v. 41; and to Nathanael, v. 45) and to that of the Gentiles (to the Greeks of 12:20-22). It is, thus, thanks to the witness of the Baptist, as 1:7 predicts, that all—both Jews and Gentiles—come to believe in Christ.

Yet verse 43, with its breaking of the chain, still stands in the way; for here Jesus appeals directly to Philip. Facing this prob-

---

[58] M.-E. Boismard, "Les traditions johanniques concernant le Baptiste," *RB* LXX (1963), 5-42 (40).

lem, Boismard comes, finally and with admirable reserve, to the suggestion that the verse is the work of a post-Johannine redactor (who in Boismard's view is already on the scene, so to speak, being responsible for constructing the present text of 1:19-36 out of two earlier and strikingly parallel versions). Boismard remarks that his hesitancy to suggest such a solution was overcome in part when he noted that F. Spitta and W. Wilkens, without being guided by the prediction of 1:7, had already allotted verse 43 to the hand of a redactor simply on the basis of factors in that verse itself.[59] In turn, the arguments of Boismard, Spitta, and Wilkens clearly had an impact on R. Schnackenburg: "On this [redactional] hypothesis some things are easier to understand. . . ."[60] He is, nevertheless, reluctant to assign verse 43 to the redactor's hand without some indication in verse 44 that it did in fact originally follow immediately upon verses 40-42.[61]

If, now, the four problems just outlined incline one to consider the possibility of editorial activity in verse 43, yet the arguments for allotting the whole verse to the post-Johannine redactor are found inconclusive, it may be wise to ponder whether the problems did not perhaps arise at an earlier point, i.e., at the level of the evangelist's editing of his source.[62]

---

[59]*Ibid.*, p. 42, referring to F. Spitta, *Das Johannes-Evangelium* (Göttingen, 1910), p. 57 and to W. Wilkens, *Die Entstehungsgeschichte des vierten Evangeliums* (Zollikon, 1958), p. 35. The comments of both authors are well worth reading. One should also ponder Boismard's observation (thanks, apparently, to M. l'abbé Georges Roux) that the expression "Follow me" occurs in the Fourth Gospel only in 1:43 and in the redactional Chapter 21 (v. 19). Note also Boismard's more recent comments about the final redaction of the Fourth Gospel: P. Benoit and M. E. Boismard, *Synopse des Quatre Évangiles* (Paris, 1972), II, 16, 43 and *passim*.

[60]R. Schnackenburg, *The Gospel According to St. John* (London, 1968), I, 313.

[61]Presumably the case would have been acceptable to Schnackenburg if verse 44 had read somewhat as follows: "And Philip, the second of the two who had heard John, was from Bethsaida. . . ."

[62]Schnackenburg's typically sagacious comments on 1:43 form one of the points at which one wonders why, having granted some probability to the hypothesis of a signs source (*St. John* I, 67), the author does not

This is, in fact, the route elected both by Bultmann and by Fortna.[63] The latter proposes that in the source 1:43 read as follows:

And he (Andrew) found Philip.
And Jesus said to him:
"Follow me!"

He then holds the evangelist responsible for the first half of the present verse—"on the morrow . . . Galilee"—which he judges to be "an artificial insertion."

Considering the possible cogency of Fortna's analysis, one must admit, I think, that the second line follows rather abruptly on the first and that the antecedent "to him" is consequently a bit awkward. One might thus entertain doubts that Fortna has in this case recovered the whole of the source's reading, and yet be inclined to consider seriously the hypothesis that at 1:43 the source did in fact read somewhat differently from the present text. Can further analysis yield a more convincing reading?

Two literary observations intersect in a way which would seem to justify an affirmative answer. First, we may reread the whole of 1:35-49, bearing firmly in mind the Baptist's three denials (1:20f.). As is well known, this paragraph abounds in the application to Jesus of christological titles, but *literally* two of these are accented by being placed as the objects of the single verb-form "we have found," namely "the Messiah" (v. 41) and "the one of whom Moses wrote" (v. 45).[64] One notices that these

---

draw on this probability to wrestle with certain kinds of problems in the present text. The question does not arise in just the same way, of course, as one reads the commentary of Lindars, for whom the theory of two major editions largely takes the place of source criticism. One learns a great deal from Lindars' massive labors, but his specific comments on 1:43 do not seem to bring us very far forward: ". . . awkward as it is, the text can stand. . . . In any case the verse is only aimed at bringing Philip onto the stage, because of his part in what follows" (*Behind the Fourth Gospel, ad loc.*).

[63]Bultmann, *Johannes*, p. 68; Fortna, *Signs*, pp. 184f.

[64]Fortna, *Signs*, p. 188; for the subject of the verb in the first line, see p. 184.

accented titles correspond to the first and last of the three titles which the Baptist so dramatically denies for himself. When one also notices that our problematic verse lies precisely between these two, the suggestion virtually presents itself that the Baptist's second denial, otherwise left dangling, may have had its positive counterpart in the original wording of verse 43:

| *Three Denials* | *Three (?) Affirmations* |
|---|---|
| 20. I am not the Christ | 41. We have found the Messiah |
| 21. Are you Elijah? . . . I am not | 43. (We have found Elijah)? |
| 21. Are you the prophet? . . . No | 45. The one of whom Moses wrote . . . we have found |

Second, and rather more weighty, I think, is the observation that verses 41f. and 45-47 evidence a remarkable degree of structural similarity which may be represented as follows:[65]

---

[65] The structural similarity of verses 41f. and verses 45ff. has been frequently observed, of course, even if not always displayed in the same way. See, e.g., the analysis made by Boismard, "Les traditions," p. 41, and note the important observation by Hahn that "die Anrede ἴδε ἀληθῶς Ἰσραηλίτης ἐν ᾧ δόλος οὐκ ἔστιν in v. 47b zumindest in einer lockeren Entsprechung zu der Namensverleihung in v. 42b zu sehen [ist]" ("Die Jüngerberufung Joh. 1, 35-51," *Neues Testament und Kirche* [für Rudolf Schnackenburg], ed. J. Gnilka [Freiburg, 1974], p. 180). Strangely, however, this observation is one of the remarkably few points at which the analysis made by Hahn and that of the present essay exhibit agreement. Regarding this divergence there is space here for only four brief comments: (1) While, as always, I am instructed by several aspects of Hahn's work, (see, for example, "Der Prozess Jesu nach dem Johannesevangelium," *Evangelisch-Katholischer Kommentar zum Neuen Testament*, 3 vols. [Neukirchen, 1970], II, 23-96), I find that his analysis in this case shows the necessity to pursue in great detail the literary structure of the text before us—and hence the literary problems, including those of syntax—*before* one turns to *Formgeschichte*. This is precisely what Hahn does not do. One can only register amazement that he passes right by the vexing problems of verse 43, a procedure which is scarcely unrelated to his allotting virtually the whole of the verse as it stands to the "Grundform der Berufungserzahlung" (p. 178). (2) It is this same

*vv. 41f.*

(1) He (Andrew) *found* first his brother . . . Simon

(2) *and said to him*, "We have found the Messiah."[66]

(3) He led him to Jesus.

(4) Looking at him,

(5) *Jesus said*, "You are Simon. . . ."


*vv. 45-47*

(1) Philip *found* Nathanael

(2) *and said to him*, "The one of whom Moses wrote . . . we have found. . . ."

(3) And Nathanael said to him. . . . Philip said to him, "Come and see."

(4) *Jesus* saw Nathanael coming to him, and

(5) he *said* about him, "Behold, truly an Israelite. . . ."[67]

---

electing of *Formgeschichte* prior to a detailed literary analysis which enables Hahn to speak of verse 43 as evidencing a useful parallelism to the Synoptic *Berufungsgeschichten*. In spite of the absence of the third expected element, the *Vollzugsbericht*, Hahn locates the expected *Situationsbeschreibung* in Jesus' finding of Philip and the expected *Berufungswort* in the brief call "Follow me!" About the latter point there is no debate. The call is certainly traditional. As regards the former, however, Hahn fails to observe the facts about the verb "to find": (a) It is used in none of the Synoptic *Berufungsgeschichten*. (b) It provides one of the major characteristics of the present passage (five times in five verses). Hence this verb ties verse 43 not to the *Synoptic* form of the *Berufungsgeschichte*, but rather to its present context. The distinction is crucial to the literary analysis, and, if it is taken into account, one will scarcely identify Jesus' finding of Philip as a pre-Johannine *Situationsbeschreibung*. (3) Hahn is surely correct to point out two rather different pictures in the paragraph. In verse 43 it is Jesus who takes the initiative, making a man into his disciple by means of his authoritative word. In verses 41, 42a, and 45f. it is, on the other hand, not Jesus himself, but rather one of his disciples who issues the call. In Hahn's opinion, both of these pictures have come to John from tradition. On the face of it, that is, of course, entirely possible, especially if one leaves aside a detailed analysis of the problems presented by the present wording of verse 43. Even so, a warning signal would certainly arise from careful consideration of such passages as 5:14; 6:44, 65; 15:16; and 9:35, all of which seem clearly to come from the evangelist. In light of these passages, one could at least ask whether the picture in which Jesus takes the initiative (present form of verse 43) may not stem from the evangelist.

Now, if one recalls the four vexing problems of verse 43 as it is presently worded, if one entertains seriously the possibility that these problems may have arisen as a result of editorial activity on the part of the evangelist, if one bears in mind the suggestion that the second of the Baptist's denials may have had some kind of positive counterpart in the original wording of this problematic verse, and if, finally, the form of verses 41f. and 45-47 should lead one to credit the author of the source with a good sense for parallel structuring, it is surely no huge step to the hypothesis that in the source the verse read somewhat as follows, showing the same five-membered structure:

---

The fact that it contains *one* traditional clause "Follow me!" should scarcely lead one to assign it *in its present form* to pre-Johannine tradition. (4) Finally, there is the weighty theological issue of the nature of the call to discipleship. At the end of his article, Hahn has some words about this issue which seem to me both perceptive and puzzling. Since he believes that the evangelist has developed verses 45f. out of verses 41 and 42a, it is not greatly surprising that he finds the evangelist's own concern to be expressed in the *indirekte Berufung* of these verses rather than in the *direkte Berufung* of verse 43: "Er [der Evangelist] wollte damit der Situation der Jünger in einer Zeit gerecht werden, in der die *indirekte Berufung* in die Nachfolge längst an die Stelle der direkten getreten war. . . ." (p. 190, italics added). In light of 6:44, 65, etc. (see above), this statement seems to me to stand the matter exactly on its head; and I cannot avoid wondering whether Hahn does not at some level realize that; for his final words are: ". . . denn wie immer sich die Nachfolge vollzieht, *die unmittelbare Begegnung* mit dem lebendigen Herrn ist das Herzstück christlicher Jüngerschaft" (p. 190, italics added). Regarding John 4:39-42, another passage which could come under consideration, see H. Leroy, *Rätsel und Misverständnis* (Bonn, 1968), pp. 92ff., and the comment below in note 83.

[66] It would be the evangelist, of course, who provides the interpretation of the term "Messiah"; cf. Fortna, *Signs*, p. 184.

[67] Verses 45-47 paint a somewhat more detailed picture than do verses 41f., but the essential structure is strikingly similar. I have underlined "Jesus" in line 4 because it clearly goes with the verb "he said" in line 5. Note moreover "to Jesus" in line 3 of verses 41f., and compare with "to him" in line 4 of verses 45-47. Compare also "looking at" with "he saw."

*v. 43*

(1) He (Andrew secondly)[68] *found* Philip

(2) *and said to him*, "We have found Elijah who comes to restore all things [or some such]."

(3) He led Philip to Jesus [or some such].

(4) And, looking at him,

(5) *Jesus said*, "Follow me!"[69]

*Voilà!* A direct facing of the problems of verse 43, notably the break in the witness/discovery chain, and a structural analysis of the surrounding verses have led us to hypothesize that John's source for 1:19ff. and 1:35ff. and at least five of the miracle stories did in fact contain—between the Baptist's denial that he is Elijah and the Elijah-like portrait of Jesus—exactly what we have been watching for, an explicit identification of Jesus as Elijah.

It would be dishonest of me to say that I consider this hypothesis to be extremely tenuous. On the contrary, it seems to me to enjoy a considerable  egree of probability.[70] Nevertheless, I am bound to face the question whether the emergence of this line of thought is a case of watching for something so intently that one finds it by hypothesizing it into existence without adequate

---

[68] I have placed these two words in parenthesis because of the difficulty of deciding whether the likelihood lies with Andrew or with Peter.

[69] One should not be greatly surprised to note that the weighty Christian interpretation of the verb "to follow" (see E. Schweizer's classic *Lordship and Discipleship* [Naperville, 1960]) emerges on all three levels in the Fourth Gospel: the signs source (1:37; 1:40; apparently 1:43), the evangelist's own composition (8:12; 13:36; etc.), and the work of the post-Johannine redactor (21:19ff.). That the verb is traditionally used in stories of Jesus' call to discipleship leads Hahn (n. 65 above) to assign 1:43 to a pre-Johannine, Synoptic-like tradition; that the formula "Follow me!" occurs in 21:19 caused Boismard (in 1963) to assign 1:43 to a post-Johannine redactor; the presence of the verb in the context of 1:43, in verses assigned by Fortna to the source, inclines me to think that it was used by the author of the source in his form of 1:43.

[70] Not least because, as I have indicated above (n. 43), the present study began not at all as a quest for a confession of Jesus as Elijah, but rather as an attempt to solve the syntactical problems of 1:43.

grounds. Beyond one's judgment of the arguments advanced thus far, the answer given will depend to some degree on the results of two final questions: (1) whether the hypothetical reading of 1:43 helps us to recover a section of the source which offers a picture of the author that is coherent and both *religionsgeschichtlich* and *theologiegeschichtlich* convincing, and (2) whether, beginning with the hypothesis, one sees compelling theological reasons for thinking that the evangelist, faced with such a reading in his source, would probably have altered the text to the present wording.

## V. THE ELIJAH COMPONENT IN THE SOURCE'S CHRISTOLOGY

Following Haenchen and Fortna, I find it quite plausible to think that the source in question served as a kind of rudimentary Gospel in John's church prior to his own literary activity.[71]

---

[71] E. Haenchen, "Johanneische Probleme," *ZTK* LVI (1959), 53f. No aspect of Fortna's work has been more hotly debated than his conclusion that a single document lies behind most of John's narrative sections, including the passion, and that it should properly be termed, therefore, the Signs *Gospel.* See, e.g., J. M. Robinson's comments in J. M. Robinson and H. Köster, *Trajectories Through Early Christianity* (Philadelphia, 1971), pp. 247-249. It would be foolish for me to think that in a footnote I can add anything significant to the debate. I do want, however, to make three brief comments for clarification: (1) D. M. Smith's recent discussion of this question seems to me to warrant serious consideration (*NTS* XXI, 24f.), and one will want to attend to Fortna's latest word on the issue in "Christology in the Fourth Gospel: Redaction-Critical Perspectives," *NTS* XXI (1974-75), 17ff. (2) While I am inclined to accept Fortna's thesis in general outline, I must point out that for the present study it is a matter of inconsequence whether one links the source material behind 1:19-49 to a signs source or to a signs Gospel. (3) This last point could be questioned, to be sure, precisely in light of the present thesis that for the author of the source Jesus was the eschatological Elijah. Would an author be likely, so the counter-argument could run, to ask his readers to think that the Elijah who escaped death, being translated to heaven, had returned to earth in Jesus, not only miraculously to help the needy, but also to suffer and die? Hence, if one is convinced that

Whether one agrees or not, however, it seems quite clear that there is no passage allotted to the source which is more transparent to the author's intention than the one which has just drawn our attention: the traditional elements behind 1:35-49.[72] For here we find not only an amazing richness in christological titles—Lamb of God, Messiah, *ex hypothesi* Elijah, Mosaic prophet, Son of God, and King of Israel—reflecting, no doubt, the author's concentrated attention to christology, but also a *line* of christological *movement* constructed in a way which would seem to show that the author presupposes on the part of his readers certain patterns of thought not very difficult to reconstruct. To be specific, he seems to take for granted that his readers are persons who already have messianic expectations. These already-had expectations form a sort of launching pad from which issues a christological trajectory, so to speak, which finds its goal, according to the author, in Jesus of Nazareth.[73] One of the central verbs is "to find" (twice in v. 41, once and *ex hypothesi* twice in v. 43, and twice in v. 45). To the centrality of this verb it corresponds that the portrait of Jesus in this paragraph is remarkably passive. He *walks* by (v. 36); he *responds* to persons who themselves are responding not to him, but to the words and acts of others (vv. 38, 42, 43 [as reconstructed], 47); these others speak and act *not because Jesus has himself commissioned them to do so*, but

---

John 1:43 originally made the Elijah identification, would it not follow that it was most likely a link in a document which consisted solely of miracle stories? This is a point at which the Coptic Elijah apocalypse emerges as pertinent, for it shows clearly that it was not ruled out, in our general period, to think of the eschatological Elijah as coming to earth only to experience suffering and death (and resurrection!). See the Coptic *Apocalypse of Elijah*, paragraph 42 (Akhmimic); G. Steindorff, "Die Apokalypse des Elias," *TU* XVII, no. 3a (1899), 169, kindly translated for me by Holland Hendrix.

[72] For reasons which cannot be developed here, I believe the evangelist authored 1:50 as a transition from the source to the Son of Man *logion* of 1:51.

[73] For what Robinson and Köster have called "trajectory," with qualifications (*Trajectories*, p. 14), Fortna helpfully proposes "direction of flow" (*NTS* XXL, n. 4). For what I am describing in the source's christology, however, "trajectory" seems the appropriate term.

rather because they stand as links in a (Baptist) chain of witness-bearing and discovery which ties traditional christological titles to the remarkably passive figure of Jesus. As it stands in the source, this paragraph should not be titled "Jesus *Calls* the First Disciples" (although Jesus' call forms a subordinate note), but rather "Some Jews Begin To *Find* the One Pointed-To in Their Expectations." Only at the end, in verse 48, does Jesus significantly qualify the line of christological movement from traditional expectations to discoveries of fulfillment by informing Nathanael that his knowledge of him anteceded Philip's calling of him. This qualification must be given its due weight; in particular it may have special import for the evangelist. The fact remains that even here it is Philip and not Jesus who calls Nathanael.

It seems reasonable to assume, therefore, that the author of the source writes both for confirmed members of his Church and for Jews whom he views as potential converts. He presupposes that the latter are persons who have long treasured in their hearts various elements of messianic expectation. He therefore allows them first to hear the Baptist deny for himself three key titles; then he allows them to behold a chain of Jews, expectant like themselves, proceeding to discover the fulfillment of their messianic hopes not in the Baptist,[74] but rather in Jesus of Nazareth, a man who is the Messiah, the eschatological Elijah, and the Mosaic prophet.[75] As the Messiah, Jesus is also the Son of God, and is so confessed, both here—by Nathanael—and at the climactic terminus of the source preserved in 20:30f. But before the author brings his document to that climax, he presents a series of miracle stories designed to follow the confessions of 1:42, 43, and 45 by presenting to his Jewish readers a rich portrait of Jesus as

---

[74] Bammel holds, interestingly, that his source Z ends with John 10:41 and its emphatic note that the Baptist did no sign (*Miracles*, 193ff.).

[75] Following an oral suggestion kindly made by Fortna, I am inclined to think that the rather strange construction of 1:45b may have resulted from the evangelist's adding to his source the words "and the prophets." Assuming that he suppressed the identification with Elijah in 1:43, one may guess that he felt it appropriate to append in verse 45 these words which somehow round out the picture without reintroducing what he wants to suppress.

the one who was in fact the Mosaic prophet, the eschatological Elijah, and the Messiah. The author, far from being suspicious of the line of christological movement which stretches from traditional expectation to discovered fulfillment, actually considers that line of movement to be the firm foundation of the good news.

To sharpen the point, one could use one's imagination to compose a text expressive of the author's missionary horizon, in order to compare it with such a text which appears in the Pauline corpus:

> They from of old who await in hope shall see, and they who search the Scriptures shall find the Messiah. (The author of the source)

> They who have never been told of him shall see, and they who have never heard of him shall understand. (Paul quoting Is. 52:15 in Rom. 15:21)

In short, the author of the source, however clearly he may write for Christian readers, seems also to represent what Paul calls "the Gospel of the circumcision."[76] For our present concern the major point is that one would scarcely be surprised to find such an author holding to the conviction that one element in the Gospel for the circumcision is the discovery on the part of Jews that their longing for the coming of the great helper and restorer—the eschatological Elijah—finds its rest in Jesus of Nazareth.[77]

---

[76] As far as I can see, neither the literary evidence employed for the study of Jewish Christianity by such authors as J. Daniélou, H. J. Schoeps, and A. F. J. Klijn, nor the archeological data collected by B. Bagatti and P. E. Testa have shown it to be a Jewish Christian motif to identify Jesus as Elijah. Such silence certainly does not help the hypothesis being pursued here; but neither does it damage the hypothesis, if one bears in mind that our attempts to reconstruct the history and thought of Jewish Christianity are being made, thus far, on the basis of data which put us in touch with a *very* small fraction of the original picture(s)—shall we say one-tenth or one-onehundredth?

[77] Referring to the copious discussion of recent years on the question of the Gospel *Gattung* and the possible pertinence of Greco-Roman

## VI. The Johannine Redaction

A full exploration of the hypothesis as regards the evangelist's redaction of the form of 1:43, which he found in the source, would take us far beyond the necessary limits of the present essay; for we would need in that case comprehensively and in

---

aretalogies, R. E. Brown aptly remarks: "If the Elijah and Elisha cycles of miracles had been composed in Greek in the second century B.C., with the name of a Greek god substituted for Yahweh, I suspect that these cycles would be classified by scholars as aretalogies and would be singled out as the closest analogues to the collected miracles of Jesus of Nazareth. But since they are eighth- and seventh-century Hebrew miracle collections, they do not enter much of this discussion about pre-Gospel aretalogies" (*Perspective* 12, 97). See also Reim, *Studien*, pp. 206ff.; and recall two pertinent remarks made by Bultmann in his commentary. Noting that some of the Baptist's disciples surely became members of the Christian Church, Bultmann continues, "That the Evangelist himself belonged to such disciples is probable, for that would make understandable his use of Baptist tradition. The paragraph of 1:35-51 would show, then, that the Evangelist had been converted through such disciples of the Baptist who themselves had become Christian before him. The source which he employs in this paragraph had its origin in the propaganda which such persons formulated in behalf of Christian faith" (*Johannes*, p. 78 and n. 6 there). Two pages later we find another comment which may be pertinent to the question of Gospel *Gattung*. Noting that two of the miracles in the pre-Johannine source are numbered, Bultmann poses a question and cites a relevant datum: "Was it already a practice in Judaism to number the Old Testament miracles and place them in a series? Compare *Yoma 29a* (Billerbeck, *Kommentar*, II, 409f.): Rabbi Asi (ca. 300) said: Esther is the conclusion of all [OT] miracles" (*Johannes*, p. 78, no. 4). It hardly needs to be added that these helpfully provocative observations of Brown and Bultmann should not be interpreted as favoring a "Jewish" milieu for the source as to a "Hellenistic" one. One hopes it will soon be common knowledge that the Judaism of New Testament times—with all of its manifold variations—was itself, to one degree or another, a Hellenistic religion. Regarding a dominant strain in the *religionsgeschichtliche* aspects of Nicol, *Sēmeia*, Meeks is, I think, fully justified in speaking sharply: " . . . Nicol is so determined to show that there is nothing 'Hellenistic' about the signs source that he falls into an incredibly wooden and confused use of the categories "Hellenistic' and 'Jewish.' Consequently the second chapter is an anachronism in research today" (" 'Am I a Jew?' Johannine Christianity and Judaism," in *Christianity, Judaism, and Other Greco-Roman Cults* I [Leiden, 1975], p. 184, n. 82).

great detail to consider the broad picture of his redactional activity in the whole of the first chapter and beyond.[78] In the present context, we must limit ourselves to a few observations which bear directly on the degree of probability one may grant to the hypothesis.

## A. The Literary Dimensions

The literary dimensions of the editing required by the hypothesis may be easily grasped simply by returning to the text proposed for the source:

(1) He (Andrew secondly) found Philip
(2) and *said* to him, "We have found Elijah who comes to restore all things."
(3) He led Philip to Jesus.
(4) And, looking at him,
(5) *said* Jesus, "Follow me!"

An author concerned to suppress the identification of Jesus with Elijah would have little difficulty altering this text to that end. There are two instances of the verb "he said" (lines 2 and 5), and the Elijah identification lies between the two. It would be easy, therefore, simply to delete the intervening material by passing from the first "he said" to the second:

(1) He (Andrew secondly) found Philip
(2) and said to him . . .
(3) . . .
(4) . . .
(5) . . . Jesus, "Follow me!"

---

[78] It is obvious that the major motivation for studies such as the present one may properly lie in the possibility of employing redaction criticism in order to bring the evangelist's own theology more clearly into focus. Two qualifications, however, are in order. The first is that of time and space, already mentioned. The second is the need to broaden our understanding of lines of development in early Christian thought and life. The fact that the Church did not canonize the source with its inclusion of an "Elijah christology" cannot in itself assure us that the latter has no theological value.

An author who wanted, in addition, to provide a travel notice in preparation for the story of Chapter 2 would perhaps elect to do so at a point at which he is already making alterations. Prefixing a notice of Jesus' movement to Galilee would virtually necessitate awarding the verb "he found" to Jesus—picturing the events is difficult enough, even with Jesus as the subject of all three finite verbs. Hence:

(0)  On the morrow[79] he wished to go to Galilee, and
(1)  he found . . . Philip
(2)  and said to him . . .
(3)  . . .
(4)  . . .
(5)  . . . Jesus, "Follow me!"

There is, to be sure, one further change which would seem to be called for: the advancing of the subject "Jesus" into line (0), either immediately before or after "he wished." While the translator of the Peshitta, sensing the syntactical difficulty, took exactly this step,[80] it is clear from the present state of the text that the author from whose hand it has come to us was not bothered by its awkwardness. *Ex hypothesi* he was satisfied to have suppressed the Elijah identification and to have introduced the travel notice, without having to go to great lengths to do so.

### B.   The Major Motivational/Theological Dimensions of John's Redaction

While a comprehensive analysis of the evangelist's redaction at 1:43 must await another setting, as I have indicated above, some exploration is in order here. I have just mentioned two redactional motives: the evangelist's apparent determination to suppress the Elijah identification, and his desire to introduce a travel notice. The latter needs no further comment in the present study. The former, by contrast, calls, of course, for concentrated attention. Before we turn to it, however, there is yet another

---

[79] See Fortna, *Signs*, p. 184: ". . . the scheme of days . . . (cf. 4:3, 43; 6:1, 7:1) is an artificial insertion by John."

[80] Noted by Bultmann, *Johannes*, p. 68, n. 3.

possible motive which deserves brief discussion. The literary clue which indicates the possibility of this motive is the evangelist's replacing of Andrew by Jesus as the subject of the verb "he found" in line (1).[81]

I have suggested above that this change is mainly a matter of the evangelist's maintaining a reasonable degree of editorial coherence. Once he has introduced the travel notice, the demands of syntactical and logical clarity lead him to allow Jesus — however awkwardly — to be the subject of "he found." This may, in fact, be the whole story. On the other hand, to change the subject of *this* verb is to make an alteration of some theological import, and it would seem unlikely that such a matter would be entirely accidental on the part of one of the subtlest theologians of the early Church. There are, moreover, reasons to think that the evangelist was quite happy to make the change.

It has two major dimensions: it alters the otherwise remarkably passive portrait of Jesus, showing him in *this* instance to take the initiative in finding a disciple;[82] and it breaks the chain of witness-discovery so fundamental to the source's christological trajectory, which arches from traditional expectations to discovered fulfillment. As regards the second of these — they are virtually opposite sides of a single coin — there are passages elsewhere in the Gospel which would seem to indicate considerable reservations on the part of the evangelist toward precisely the source's traditional christological trajectory.[83] I shall mention only one.

---

[81] I have mentioned above the possibility that in the source Peter rather than Andrew was the subject. It could also have been the unnamed disciple of verse 40. One can scarcely be very confident, nor is this an instance in which confidence greatly matters.

[82] See again the discussion of Hahn (*Neues Testament und Kirche*, 172-90) in n. 65 above.

[83] See, e.g., 5:14; 6:44, 65; 9:35; 15:16. One would certainly be tempted to cite also 4:39-42, in spite of the perceptive argument made by Leroy, *Rätsel*, pp. 92ff., for viewing that text as a deposit from Samaritans who, by the claim given there, succeeded against opposition in entering the Johannine community. If Leroy is correct, the Samaritans' success could be due to the use of a confession quite harmonious with a theological point high on the evangelist's agenda.

On the day following the feeding miracle of John 6:1ff., a group of persons emerge who are represented as harboring messianic expectations on the basis of Scripture (6:25-31). Moreover, they are obviously considering the possibility—in however prejudicial a manner—that the trajectory issuing from these traditional expectations does indeed find its goal in Jesus. It would have been quite harmonious in the scene had the narrator introduced a second group coming to the first and asking whether they had "found" the expected Messiah.

As the scene actually unfolds, however, the crowd's comments create an atmosphere quite different from that of 1:35ff. For what these people propose to do is to give Jesus a *chance* to meet their messianic expectations (6:30f.), and subsequent developments show that they do not consider him to have passed *their test* (6:41f., 52). In short, the christological trajectory so positively exemplified in the source at 1:35ff. proves here to be a debatable matter. Those who *begin* with traditional expectations believe themselves competent to preside over the question whether their expectations are fulfilled in one they consider to be a prospective *candidate*.

Faced with *this* development (one supposes it is portrayed in Chapter 6 because it somehow corresponds to actual events which have transpired since the writing of the source) the evangelist sees the necessity fundamentally to qualify the christological trajectory itself. Hence he hears Jesus speak the sharp words: "Why [like the wilderness generation] do you murmur among yourselves? No one is able to come to me [cf. "find the Messiah"] unless the Father who sent me draw him" (6:43f.; cf. 6:65).[84]

---

[84]Cf. Is. 43:18ff. and particularly Ps. 78:17ff. The latter presents an especially striking pattern. First, the wilderness generation experiences God's grace in the gift of water from the rock. One supposes they gave thanks for the welcome stream. Next, however, they proceed, so to speak, to wrench God's gracious deed out of his hand (to separate it from him) and to turn it into the genesis of a trajectory of expectation on the basis of which they themselves propose to preside over the next move. They are the ones who give God the test (v. 18) and who say, "He smote the rock so that water gushed out. . . . Can he also give bread . . . ?" (v. 20).

Returning now to 1:43, one can easily see that the evangelist's making Jesus the subject of "he found" results in a verse which similarly—though, as is appropriate in this context, non-polemically—qualifies the source's christological trajectory by placing in the midst of the witness/discovery chain one instance in which the initiative (of election) lies clearly with Jesus. Because the atmosphere created in this paragraph of the source is so positive and compelling, one would scarcely suppose, to be sure, that the evangelist altered the verse primarily in order to provide this qualification. It would seem, however, that, having decided to edit the verse for other reasons, the evangelist was happy also to seize the opportunity to reveal the gracious line which finds its beginning not in traditional expectation, but rather in God's sovereign election through Jesus Christ.[85]

We come, finally, to the heart of the evangelist's editing of 1:43, the suppression of the Elijah identification. In order to see it in perspective, we need to look briefly at the literary structure achieved by the evangelist in the first chapter.

Assuming the validity of the hypothesis, it would seem that in Chapter 1 the evangelist has taken four major steps in regard to the source: (1) he has prefixed a hymn (vv. 1ff.), which finds its focus in statements about the pre-existent logos, now become incarnate in Jesus; (2) he has completed his prologue by immediately providing on the basis of the hymn an exegesis, the climax of which includes a polemically formulated denial that anyone other than the Incarnate One has ever seen God (v. 18);

---

[85] Even in the positive and compelling atmosphere of 1:35ff., the evangelist may have qualified the source's traditional christological trajectory at one other point, verse 48. Above I have implied that this verse is to be assigned to the source. That may, indeed, be the best analysis; yet there are several reasons for seeing it, on the whole, as a redactional insertion by John. (a) However the literal call to discipleship may be issued, Jesus is shown to be the active and prescient Lord; (b) the question "how," while not always from the evangelist's hand, is often his; (c) the formula "he answered and said" has been judged to be a stylistic characteristic of the evangelist (E. Ruckstuhl, *Die literarische Einheit des Johannesevangeliums* [Freiburg, 1951], pp. 197f.). The last two of these observations were made by Fortna, and he therefore felt obliged to overcome them in order to assign 1:48 to the source (*Signs*, p. 186).

(3) he has employed from the source an account of the Baptist's witness, including his three denials, and an account of the coming of the first disciples in which he has suppressed the explicit identification of Jesus as Elijah;[86] and (4) he has provided as a climax for the chapter a highly impressive Son of Man logion (v. 51).[87] Without entering into detailed discussion, it is not difficult to see that these four steps are tightly interlocked. Whatever the precise relationship between hymn and Gospel, one thing is transparent: the evangelist has an extraordinary affinity for the hymn's christology; for his Christ is clearly the One who receives reverent witness from Abraham (8:56), Moses (5:39), and the prophets (12:41), while towering far above them in his eternal pre-existence: "I solemnly assure you, before Abraham was I am" (8:58). As the One who existed from eternity at the Father's side, he and he alone has seen the Father (1:18); he and he alone comes from above, having witnessed the heavenly glories (3:13, 31ff.); he and he alone can therefore impart the revelation of God (1:18; 3:31ff.). In his identity as the pre-existent Son of Man, he is the sole locus of communication between heaven and earth (1:51).

Could one identify this figure with Elijah? To ask the question is to answer it. The evangelist could leave Elijah-like traits strewn among the miracle stories, and very probably not merely out of reverence for his source. But he could scarcely allow the explicit identification and at the same time maintain the integrity of his own massive christology; for, in the frame of *his* christology, to do so would have implied that the logos experienced successive incarnations.[88] We can be very nearly certain that this

---

[86] In suggesting that the evangelist deliberately suppressed the Elijah identification, I find myself making a statement at variance with a goodly number of interpreters who hold either that all of the major literary layers in the Gospel represent the essentially unchanging views of a single theologian or school (R. E. Brown; B. Lindars), or that, while the evangelist employed a signs source, he did not at any point intend to contradict it (Fortna, *NTS* XXI, 26).

[87] These remarks should not be taken to imply that all of 1:19-50 comes from the source.

[88] It will be obvious, by contrast, that the evangelist was able to combine the identification of Jesus as the Mosaic prophet with his em-

latter idea never seriously presented itself to John as a usable scheme, not because it was *religionsgeschichtlich* inconceivable (note the successive incarnations of the "true prophet" in the Kerygmata Petrou), but because it would have diluted what for him could not be diluted: Jesus Christ the eternal Son as the sole mediator of God's revelation. In short, the Elijah christology of the source had to give way to the christology of eternal pre-existence, expressed initially in the figure of the logos, and then dominantly in the figure of the descending and ascending Son of Man.[89]

*Ex hypothesi*, therefore, as far as we can see, it is the fourth evangelist who bears the responsibility for the disappearance from subsequent Christian thought of the identification of Jesus as the eschatological Elijah.[90] We thus witness one of the points in history—only one of them—at which an aspect of the varied

---

phasis on Christ's pre-existence. For the major line of hope attaching itself to the Mosaic prophet looks forward to one who is *like* Moses. Hence, to identify Jesus as the Mosaic prophet is to affirm a typological relationship between two distinct figures. See Martyn, *History and Theology*.

[89] To return to the matter of the literary-theological structure of Chapter 1, we may now note that the Elijah identification is, so to speak, squeezed out of the picture between the pre-existent logos on the one side (1:18) and the pre-existent Son of Man on the other (1:51). See R. Hamerton-Kelly, *Pre-Existence, Wisdom, and the Son of Man: A Study of the Idea of Pre-Existence in the New Testament* (Cambridge, 1973), pp. 197-242. In a future study I hope to explore the implications which the Elijah identification itself may have had for the thought of pre-existence. See the comments on John 1:15, 27, and 30 in n. 45 above. Did the author of the source, having identified Jesus as the eschatological Elijah, take the additional and rather short step to the thought of pre-existence?

[90] I say "as far as we can see" because there is, of course, no strong reason to think that the identification emerged at only one point in early Christian thought, i.e., only in the mind of the Johannine source's author. It would be strange, in fact, if numerous kinfolk of persons healed by Jesus did not identify him as Elijah, as is implied in the Synoptics (Mk. 6:15, etc.). Did none of these become "Christians"? Reim *Studien*, p. 9: "We will have to reckon with an Elijah christology *within* early Christianity."

patterns of christological thinking in Jewish Christianity was suppressed. Whether that which was put in its place justifies the suppression is a question for the fully theological interpretation not only of the Fourth Gospel itself, but also of the role it has played in the subsequent history of Christian thought and life.[91] In light of the disastrous effects of the monolithic wall which the West erected against the Jewish Christians in the latter part of the second century (i.e., from Irenaeus onward), one may perhaps be permitted some degree of ambiguity, while yet recognizing the ultimacy of that christology to which Zinzendorf bore witness in his famous confession: "I have but one passion. That is he and only he."[92]

---

[91] See the studies by W. von Loewenich, *Das Johannesverständnis im zweiten Jahrhundert* (Giessen, 1932); F. M. Braun, *Jean Le Théologien et son Évangile dans l'Église ancienne* (Paris, 1959); J. N. Sanders, *The Fourth Gospel in the Early Church* (Cambridge, 1943); M. F. Wiles, *The Spiritual Gospel* (Cambridge, 1960); T. E. Pollard, *Johannine Christology and the Early Church* (London, 1970); E. Pagels, *The Johannine Gospel in Gnostic Exegesis* (Nashville, 1973); C. K. Barrett, " 'The Father Is Greater Than I (John 14:28): Subordinationist Christology in the New Testament," in *Neues Testament und Kirche,* ed. Gnika pp. 144-59.

[92] Quoted by Käsemann, *The Testament of Jesus*, p. 38. We are moving, I think, toward a more adequate understanding of the phenomenal christological concentration of the Johannine community and the particular forms it took, thanks to several recent studies mentioned in the notes; special attention is due to the masterful article by Meeks, "The Man from Heaven in Johannine Sectarianism," *JBL* XCI (1972), 44-72. Perhaps on the basis of these various studies it will even prove possible to give in general terms a history of christological thinking within the Johannine circle. c.f. U. B. Müller, *Die Geschichte der Christologie in der Johanneishen Gemeinde* (Stuttgart, 1975).

# CHAPTER 2

# Persecution and Martyrdom

**A Dark and Difficult Chapter in the
History of Johannine Christianity**

## I. POSING THE QUESTIONS

In the previous chapter we have seen grounds for positing a relationship between the Gospel of John and Jewish Christianity, primarily because the Gospel retains views of Christ characteristic of Jewish Christians. The fourth evangelist proves to have been the shaper of *christological formulations* which he inherited quite directly from Jewish-Christian sources.

The question now arises whether aspects of *ecclesiology* which emerge in his Gospel may also point in the direction of Jewish Christianity. In the present chapter we will pursue this question in a quite specific form: Would it perhaps be the case that certain experiences of the Johannine community indicate it to have been itself a Jewish-Christian church at one point in its history?

When one ponders this question, two strands in the Fourth Gospel come dominantly to mind. The first strand consists of those passages which announce that Jews who confess Jesus to be the Messiah are expelled from the synagogue (9:22; 12:42; 16:2). Excommunication from the synagogue for messianic confession of Jesus would clearly be an experience peculiar to Jewish Christians. In the present context I shall take for granted both that basic point and my own earlier analysis of the factors involved (see Chapters One and Two of *History and Theology in the Fourth Gospel,* revised and enlarged edition, Abingdon, 1979). On that ground alone we are able to answer our question in the affirmative. At the very beginning of its existence as a community separate to itself, the Johannine church must have been Jewish-Christian in nature.

We may still ask, however, whether it existed as such *for some period of time*; and when we pose the question in this way, we are reminded of a second strand in the Gospel which indicates that Jews who believe in Jesus may be subjected not only to expulsion from the synagogue, but also to severe discipline and indeed to persecution which goes as far as death:

> I have told you these things (that the world will hate you) to keep you from being shaken in your faith. They are going to excommunicate you from the synagogue. Indeed the hour is coming when the man who puts you to death will believe that in doing so he is offering an act of service to God! (16:2)

We are not told much about this man who persecutes to the death, except that he understands his activity to be an act of worshipful service to God. In light of the fact that the horrible and heinous and centuries-long persecution of Jews by Christians has sometimes been "justified" by the theory that the Jews did the first persecuting, it is understandable that a number of Christian interpreters have wished to see this verse as a reference to the persecution of Christians not by Jews, but by Roman authorities. Yet the Greek word rendered "act of (worshipful) service" refers elsewhere in the New Testament to Jewish worship, and the other experience referred to in this text, excommunication from the synagogue, points to the action of Jewish authorities. Modern relations between Jews and Christians are not helped by an antihistorical interpretation of biblical texts. I have argued elsewhere that for the Johannine community this additional experience of ultimate persecution was also experienced at the hands of Jewish authorities (Chapters Three and Four of *History and Theology*). What needs now to be further pursued is the question whether we are thereby speaking of an experience of the Johannine community during a period in which it *remained a Jewish*-Christian church.

A major line of investigation could perhaps open up were we to inquire whether the particular kind of deadly persecution reflected in John 16:2 (and 7:45-52) may also be reflected in sources we know to come from Jewish-Christian churches. The posing of this question will obviously lead us to ascertain whether there are Jewish-Christian sources which reflect the same kind of persecution at the hands of Jewish authorities. One thinks first of all to ask whether the New Testament itself may contain what we need. But as a matter of fact in their *present form* the books of the New Testament are virtually without exception products of Gentile Christianity; and while there are points in them at which Jewish-Christian tradition peeks through, none of these provides a picture of persecution which is strikingly and helpfully similar to that which emerges in the pertinent Johannine passages.

There are, however, a few invaluable sources for the study of Jewish Christianity which lie outside the New Testament, and one of these contains material which may indeed provide illuminating points of comparison. This Jewish-Christian source is now embedded in the so-called Pseudo-Clementine literature. Because this literature is not widely known, it will be well to pause for a word of introduction before we study the pertinent texts.

## II. A JEWISH-CHRISTIAN SOURCE
### IN THE PSEUDO-CLEMENTINES

The Pseudo-Clementine literature consists of a romance preserved in two parallel yet distinct editions called the *Homilies* and the *Recognitions*. Both of these received their present forms in the fourth century, but they draw on the common basis of a romance written in the third century, and it in turn was written by someone who employed sources penned in the second century.[93]

---

[93]The best overview of the history of research on the Pseudo-Clementines is given in the first chapter of G. Strecker, *Das Judenchristentum in den Pseudoklementinen* (Berlin, 1958; revised edition expected soon). In the Tübingen school the Pseudo-Clementines were judged to be the single most important document for understanding the post-apostolic age. Incorrect and tendentious as this judgment was, the seminal labors on the Pseudo-Clementines proved, in fact, to be those of F. C. Baur, who, in his characteristic way, succeeded—partly by indirection—in

The basic story is the familiar one of a promising youth who moves from one philosophy/religion to another in his quest for truth, coming finally to Christianity. In the present case the youth is represented to be Clement of Rome, and the major part of the romance is given over to his travels with Peter and in fact to lengthy and sometimes tedious disputes between Peter and Simon Magus. In most of the material which constitutes the romance itself we are faced with an obvious fiction penned, as I said above, not by Clement of Rome (fl. 95 A.D.), but by an unknown literary figure of the third century who drew on a number of earlier sources and who wrote long passages which have caused numerous readers to lay his text aside out of sheer boredom.

---

posing the two driving questions for subsequent research: Are the Pseudo-Clementines pertinent for the study of Jewish Christianity? Is it possible carefully to distinguish literary layers, so as to recover discrete and approximately datable sources? Vis-à-vis these questions, subsequent studies have tended to flow along two rather distinct lines: (1) John Chapman, "On the Date of the Clementines," *ZNW* 7 (1908) 21ff., 147ff., and Eduard Schwartz, "Unzeitgemässe Beobachtungen," *ZNW* 31 (1932), are the major interpreters who answered both of Baur's questions in the negative, and J. Irmscher has voiced a similar position in the current scene, "The Pseudo-Clementines," pp. 532-535 in Hennecke-Schneemelcher, *New Testament Apocrypha* II (Philadelphia, 1965). One should note also the caution represented in J. A. Fitzmyer's article, "The Qumran Schools, the Ebionites, and Their Literature," *Theol. Studies* 16 (1955) 335-372 (349). (2) Hans Waitz, *Die Pseudoklementinen, Homilien und Rekognitionen. Eine quellenkritische Untersuchung* (1904, *TU* 25, 4), on the other hand, answered both questions decisively in the affirmative, following to some extent A. Hilgenfeld, and while his work had some identifiable flaws, its main lines have proven widely convincing. One may see its influence, to mention two examples, in the dissertation of O. Cullmann, *Le problème littéraire et historique du roman pseudo-clementin* (Paris, 1930), and in the highly valuable and often aggravating study of H.-J. Schoeps, *Theologie und Geschichte des Judenchristentum* (Tübingen, 1949). The major heir of Waitz on the current scene is Georg Strecker, who has helpfully and creatively reviewed, refined, corrected, and extended Waitz's labors. Broad skepticism as to the possibility of Clementine source analysis seems to me to be quite unwarranted; and two of the sources resulting from such analysis do in fact prove to be quite pertinent to the study of second-century Jewish Christianity. See comments below on the *Kerygmata Petrou* and the *Ascents of James*.

One sparkling exception lies before us in the first book of the *Recognitions* (the text of R 1, 33-71 is provided in the Appendix). While the early chapters of Book One merely present the initial elements necessary for the Clementine romance, chapter 27 (R 1, 27) begins a substantial section which is unrelated to the romance and which has a kind of integrity not matched in the preceding dialogue material. This section is made up of what one might call two historical accounts. The first, that of R 1, 27-32, rests on a source which traced God's dealing with the world and man from creation through (at least) the twenty-first generation, that of Abraham. This source was surely written by a Jew who, in a quite straightforward way, referred to Abraham as the one "from whom our Hebrew nation is derived" (R 1, 32, 1). It is therefore not Jewish-Christian, but rather simply Jewish.

As to the remaining account, R 1, 33ff., it may be of significance not only that it begins precisely where the redemptive-historical sketch in Stephen's speech takes its beginning (Acts 7:2ff.), but also that it runs somewhat parallel to it: Abraham, Isaac, Jacob, the twelve patriarchs, the seventy-five (Acts) or seventy-two (R) who entered Egypt, and Moses, together with Moses' promise that God would raise up another prophet like him. Noting this degree of similarity, one also observes numerous instances of literary dependence on the text of canonical Acts. Clearly the author of R 1, 33ff. had the text of canonical Acts before him. More of that presently. If this literary piece begins at R 1, 33, where does it end?

Its terminus, as far as the piece is preserved in the Clementines, would seem clearly to lie at the end of R 1, 71, where the Clement romance once again emerges with a portrait of Peter lodging in the house of Zacchaeus in Caesarea, while readying himself for the disputation with Simon Magus. In between R 1, 33 and R 1, 71 there is clearly one sizable insertion from a later hand, but we are on solid ground in the assumption that we have before us in R 1, 33-71 (less the insertion in R 1, 44, 4—1, 53, 3) a literary piece penned by someone who desired to provide a sketch of redemptive history from Abraham to the early years of the Jerusalem church. Of course the presence of one insertion should warn us that there may be others, and indeed Georg Strecker has advanced good arguments for so considering the whole of chapter 63, as well as R 1, 69, 6-7 and some other snippets.[94] Qualified in this way, R 1, 33-71 presents us, I think, with a discrete literary piece.[95] Indeed, following a line of suggestions stretching all the way back to J. Köstlin (1849), Strecker has provided a strong case for identifying this literary piece not only as one of the basic sources for the Clementine romance, but also specifically as a form of the *Ascents of James* mentioned by Epiphanius.[96] A number of scholars expert in the study of Jewish Christianity hold this view, and its probability will be assumed as we proceed.[97] R 1, 33-71 (less R 1, 44, 4—1, 53, 3, etc.) is surely a discrete literary piece antedating the author of the romance, and very probably a form of the *Ascents of James*. The reader will follow our further explorations rather easily if he will pause here to read the text as it is given in the Appendix.

These literary conclusions enable us, now, to move a step further by asking who penned this historical sketch and in what setting.

One begins to attack this question by noting that the author of our source emphasizes two points of distinction as regards the Jerusalem church. The true line of religion, he tells his readers, extends from Abraham through Moses and Moses' greater successor to the Jerusalem church led by James. As the embodiment of true religion, that church is distinguished on the one side from the errors of non-Christian Judaism, and on the other from the falsity of Paulinism. (Small wonder that Matthew is the author's favorite Gospel.)

With regard to the first of these, the author explicitly says

---

[94] Strecker, *Judenchristentum*, pp. 42f., 223-250.

[95] One can survey its contents quite readily in Strecker, *Judenchristentum*, pp. 223-250.

[96] Epiphanius, *Panarion* 30, 16, 6-9 [A. F. J. Klijn and G. J. Reinink, *Patristic Evidence for Jewish-Christian Sects* (Leiden, 1973), p. 184]; Strecker, *Judenchristentum*, pp. 251-253. For the reasons advanced by Strecker I shall follow him in designating this source as the *Ascents*.

[97] See, for example, M. Simon, "La migration à Pella, Légende ou réalité?" *Judéo-christianisme, RSR* 60 (1972; Daniélou Festschrift) 49, and Klijn and Reinink, *Evidence*, pp. 81, 282.

that the Jerusalem church differs from "the unbelieving Jews" in *one point only*: the confession of Jesus as the Christ (R 1, 43, 2). With this it is harmonious that he does not speak a single word against circumcision. Indeed, it is doubtless an important clue to the character of the author's own church that he paints a picture in which Christian baptism emerges as a replacement for the sacrificial cult of the Jerusalem temple.[98] We may assume, I think, that the author belongs to a community which practices both circumcision and Christian baptism, and which is therefore made up of circumcised, baptized Jewish Christians.[99]

On the other side he is clearly concerned to distinguish the line extending through the Jerusalem church to his own community from the line represented in the development of Pauline Christianity. In all probability he included in his document a narrative of the Damascus conversion of Paul, but unfortunately that part of his work is not preserved.[100] In the material we have, Paul appears only in his pre-Christian role as the persecutor of the Church. Even here, however, two notes in particular would seem to indicate that the author intends to discredit Pauline Christianity.

1. Until Paul interferes in the temple, the mission to the Jews is enjoying phenomenal success (R 1, 69-70). By preaching for seven successive days (!), James has persuaded "all the people and the high priest" that they should be baptized (R 1, 69, 8). It is precisely at this point of unprecedented success that Paul enters and derails "what had been arranged with much labor" (R 1, 70, 4). Thus Paul is the enemy of the Jewish mission. Apart from his activity, that mission would presumably have been fantastically successful. Of course Paul is at this point not a Christian of any sort whatever. I am simply observing that our author presents

---

[98] R 1, 39, and R 1, 55; Strecker, *Judenchristentum*, pp. 228f.; cf. also pp. 141, 196ff.

[99] Vis-à-vis the mass of non-Christian Jews he seems, in fact, to use the terms "the rite of sacrifice" and "the baptism of Jesus" as equivalent expressions respectively for Judaism and Jewish Christianity; see e.g., R 1, 55.

[100] See R 1, 71; cf. Strecker, *Judenchristentum*, p. 253; Schoeps, *Theologie und Geschichte*, pp. 452f.

Paul's activity as the chief cause of a failure in the Jewish mission, and I am suggesting that he may have done this because he feels that Pauline Christianity has played exactly that role. The author would have his readers believe that had Paul and his churches never materialized, the mission of the Jewish church to its brethren would have been invincible.

2. It is doubtless significant that the author portrays Paul as the enemy, in the first instance, of James, and only in a secondary way as the enemy of Peter. For when he introduces James as the one whom the Lord ordained to be bishop over the Church of the Lord constituted in Jerusalem (R 1, 43, 3), he surely means that James represents Jewish Christianity. By the same token, he allows Paul indirectly to represent his own mission, and that mission is the enemy. To be sure, the author knows of and endorses the general mission to the Gentiles (R 1, 42, 1). It is only the specifically Pauline line which he identifies as unquestionably false.

From these two points of distinction, then, we reach a conclusion of great importance for our present concern. There is, in fact, no section of the Clementine literature about whose origin in Jewish Christianity one may be more certain.[101] The author of the *Ascents* is a Jewish Christian, a member of a church which is itself a Jewish-Christian church. On the one side stands the community of Judaism and on the other the churches of the Gentiles. Among the latter the Pauline churches stand as clearly in error as do the "unbelieving Jews." Indeed we may say something yet more specific about the author's setting, for one notes the presence of two references to the Pella story (R 1, 37, 2 and 1, 39, 3), the story which states that the Jerusalem church fled to Pella

---

[101] From the very beginning of scientific attempts at source criticism of the Clementines (Hilgenfeld), this section of R 1 has figured prominently, and it has been repeatedly recognized as being of Jewish-Christian origin. It is illuminating to compare with one another the attempts to interpret R 1 by Waitz and Strecker. Note also the all too brief remarks (pp. 256, 268) in the invaluable Appendix, "On the Problem of Jewish Christianity," which G. Strecker wrote for the revised edition of W. Bauer, *Orthodoxy and Heresy in Earliest Christianity* (Philadelphia, 1971).

in Transjordan just before or during the war of 66-70 A.D. Since that story is nowhere explicitly narrated in the New Testament (cf. Lk. 21:20ff.), we may presume that our Jewish-Christian author received it from oral tradition.[102] Moreover, since the story is of considerable importance both to him and to his readers — one notices that he can take for granted his readers' ability to understand cryptic references to it — we are surely justified in assuming that his church lies in or near Pella.[103] As to the date at which he wrote, there are good grounds for placing it near the mid-point of the second century.[104]

In studying R 1, 33-71, we are invited, therefore, to look over the shoulder, so to speak, of a Jewish-Christian writer, in or near second-century Pella, who is concerned to provide his church with the history which gives it its distinctive identity.

### III. THE JEWISH-CHRISTIAN SOURCE CALLED *THE ASCENTS OF JAMES* AND THE GOSPEL OF JOHN

The material which provides illuminating parallels to the strand in John's Gospel about deadly persecution stretches from R 1, 62 to R 1, 68. We shall make a detailed analysis momentarily. It will be profitable to approach that analysis, however, via the question whether our second-century Jewish-Christian author may be literarily dependent on the Gospel of John, for the significance of the parallels would be greatly affected by an answer to that question.

We begin by recalling that our author knew and used the canonical Acts of the Apostles. He seems in fact to have had as

---

[102] For our present purposes it is not necessary to enter into the heated debate as to whether Luke 21:20ff. reflects the Pella legend. The most one can claim is an indirect reflection. See Strecker's sharp remarks in *Judenchristentum*, p. 230, drawing on comments of Eduard Schwartz. Cf. also the article of M. Simon mentioned in note 97 above, where the views of Munck, Strecker, and Brandon are summarized and criticized.

[103] Strecker, *Judenchristentum*, p. 253.

[104] Strecker, *Judenchristentum*, pp. 253f.

one of his major concerns to stand Luke's heroic portrait of Paul exactly on its head. The Pauline mission, far from being paradigmatic of God's way with all of humankind (so canonical Acts), is one of the two major paths of error, the other being Judaism *per se*. True religion has been preserved in the Jerusalem church of James and in its progeny, such as the church of Pella.[105] Thus the author of the *Ascents* certainly intended to correct canonical Acts, and perhaps even to replace it.

It is equally clear that he knew and used several books of the Old Testament, and the Gospels of Matthew, Mark, and Luke. Indeed he shares with other Jewish Christians of the early centuries a particular love for the Gospel of Matthew, citing it quite frequently. Did he also know and draw on the Gospel of John? Two degrees of possible dependence are to be distinguished in this regard:

## A. Did the Jewish-Christian author of the *Ascents of James* draw quotations from the Gospel of John?

Interpreters have located five passages which come into question as possibly containing quotations drawn from John:

### 1. *R 1, 40, 2*

With the coming of the Mosaic prophet in Jesus,[106] the people refused to believe. Indeed they added blasphemy to their unbelief, saying that he was a gluttonous man (*voracem hominem*) and a belly slave (*ventri servientem*), and that he was

---

[105] Whether the church of Pella was historically an heir of the Jerusalem church or only understood itself to be such is a question that may remain unattended in the present context. See Strecker's arguments, *Judenchristentum*, pp. 227, 229-231, and M. Simon's article cited above in note 97. Cf. also A. Spijkerman, "An Unknown Coin-Type of Pella Decapolis, *Studii Biblici Franciscani Liber Annus* 20 (1970) 353-358, and B. Bagatti, *The Church from the Circumcision* (Jerusalem, 1971) pp. 7f.

[106] Another source behind the Pseudo-Clementines, the *Kerygmata Petrou*, speaks of the "True Prophet." See Strecker, *Judenchristentum*, pp. 223f., 145-153.

activated by a demon (*daemone agi eum*). The first two of these charges are surely drawn from Matthew 11:19 (a glutton and a drunkard; cf. Mt. 9:14). The third could stand on John 7:20 (You have a demon), as a footnote in the critical edition of the text suggests (see the Appendix). Since the first two are taken from Matthew 11:19, however, one would want to ponder whether it is not more probable that the third is drawn from the preceding verse, Matthew 11:18 (He has a demon, referring to John the Baptist), it being the case that the Synoptic tradition about Jesus' being possessed by the prince of demons (Mk. 3:22 and parallels) has enabled the author to employ both Matthew 11:18 and 11:19 as charges against Jesus himself. The very most one could say is that John 7:20 could be somewhere in the background. The slimness of that possibility is reflected, I think, in the fact that neither of the previous commentators (Waitz and Strecker) mentions it.[107]

## 2. *R 1, 43, 1*

This is one of the passages affirming the often repeated request of the Jewish authorities for a discussion with the apostles, the proposed topic being the question whether Jesus was the prophet whom Moses foretold, who is the eternal Christ (*qui est Christus aeternus*). The possibility of dependence on John 12:34 has been suggested in the critical edition of the text. The thought of the Messiah's eternity is, however, much too widespread to allow us to move beyond mere possibility.[108] Previous commentators have left us no guidance.

## 3. *R 1, 54, 5*

Describing the beliefs of the Samaritans, the author comments that from the predictions of Moses they rightly expect the prophet. The critical edition of the text mentions John 4:25, but

---

[107] Unspecified references to Waitz and Strecker pertain to their Pseudo-Clementine monographs (see note 93 above).

[108] Cf. Raymond E. Brown, *John* I, 469; Barnabas Lindars, *The Gospel of John* (London, 1972), pp. 434f.

the cited aspect of Samaritan theology was quite widely known and cannot, therefore, be used to indicate dependence on the Johannine text.[109] Again previous commentators are silent.

## 4. *R 1, 45, 4*

Christ was the Son of God and the beginning of all things (*initium omnium*); yet he became man (*homo factus est*). The possibility of dependence on John 1:1 and 1:14 shades over into probability, I think, but the passage falls in the large insertion made by the author of the romance (R 1, 44, 4—1, 53, 3). This tells us, in fact, something which we must bear in mind: It is probable that the author of the romance drew on the Fourth Gospel—at least this once—in editing the *Ascents*.

## 5. *R 1, 69, 5*

This is the crucial passage as regards the question whether our Jewish-Christian author ever quoted from John's Gospel; for it is the last, and the preceding ones have brought no more than vague possibilities. It falls in the speech made by James. After the author has given a rather full account of the speech, we find the following:

(5) And when he had plainly taught the people concerning these things, he added this also: that unless a man is baptized in water, in the name of the threefold blessedness, as the True Prophet taught, he can neither receive remission of sins nor enter into the kingdom of heaven; and he declared that this is the prescription of the unbegotten God. (6) To which he added this also: 'Do not think that we speak of two unbegotten Gods. . . . (7) But we speak of the only-begotten Son of God . . . and in like manner we speak of the Paraclete.' (8) But when he had spoken some things also concerning baptism, through seven successive days he persuaded all the

---

[109] See particularly Meeks, *The Prophet-King*, pp. 216ff., and the bibliographical references there.

people and the high priest that they should hasten immediately to receive baptism.

I have given a detailed discussion of this text elsewhere.[110] Here I shall say only that it is literarily complex, revealing the hands of our Jewish-Christian author and perhaps two later editors. If there is dependence on John 3:5, that must be credited to one of the later editors. With this observation we are led to conclude—with Hans Waitz[111] and apparently with Georg Strecker[112]—that as far as the *Ascents* has been preserved, it does not present a single quotation from the Fourth Gospel to accompany those drawn from Matthew and Luke.

### B. Did our Jewish-Christian author occasionally allude to the Gospel of John?

Even if our author did not quote from the Fourth Gospel, he may have left clues of some other sort which indicate a dependence on it. Are there perhaps motifs which are found both in the Fourth Gospel and in the *Ascents*, and which are presented in the *Ascents* in such a way as to indicate Johannine influence? Previous interpreters have weighed three arguments which would be advanced in support of this hypothesis.

1. One notices that the identification of Jesus as the prophet foretold by Moses plays a weighty role in the *Ascents* (R 1, 36, 2; 37, 2; 37, 3; 39, 1; 39, 3; 40, 4; 41, 2; 43, 1). As is well known, this motif occupies an important place in the Fourth Gospel (e.g.,

---

[110] In the original form of the present study. See notably A. J. Bellinzoni, *The Sayings of Jesus in the Writings of Justin Martyr* (Leiden, 1967), pp. 134ff.

[111] Waitz, *Pseudoklementinen*, p. 361; "The New Testament citations do not reflect even distant awareness of the Gospel of John; they contain only words and allusions which belong to the circle of the Synoptic Gospels."

[112] Strecker, *Judenchristentum*, p. 253: In discussing the literary activity of the author of the *Ascents*, Strecker remarks that he draws upon Matthew, Luke, and Acts. There is no comment on the question we are pursuing: Did the author also draw on John?

1:45; 6:14; 7:40), a far more prominent place, in fact, that it occupies in the Synoptics. One also observes, however, that in R 1, 41, 2, our author has drawn the motif of the Mosaic prophet not from John, but from Acts. In short, the prophet christology underlines both our author's dependence on Acts and his identity as a Jewish Christian.[113] It is not expressed in a way which shows him to have known and drawn on the Fourth Gospel.[114]

2. The *Ascents* and the Fourth Gospel share a polemic against followers of John the Baptist. In R 1, 60, 1 (cf. R 1, 54, 8) a disciple of the Baptist asserts that his master was the Christ, and not Jesus. It is however striking that while one could hardly imagine a point more appropriate for a quotation of John 1:20f., enriched perhaps by motifs from John 1:8 and 3:28ff., the author of the *Ascents* provides not so much as an allusion.

3. In R 1, 57, there is a reference to the issue whether worship of God takes place in Jerusalem or on Gerizim. It is a juncture at which the author could have supported his own concerns quite nicely by a quotation from—or at least an allusion to—the exchange between Jesus and the Samaritan woman in John 4: ". . . the hour is coming when neither on Gerizim nor in the Jerusalem temple will one worship the Father." Yet the author does not give even the slightest hint that Jesus ever uttered words similar to these. We thus conclude—again with Waitz and apparently with Strecker[115]—that the data we have treated thus far clearly weigh against the view which would see our second-century, Jewish-Christian author as dependent on the Fourth Gospel.

---

[113] Cf. the standard works on New Testament christology, and H.-J. Schoeps, *Theologie und Geschichte*, pp. 87ff.; R. N. Longenecker, *The Christology of Early Jewish Christianity* (Naperville, 1970), pp. 32ff.

[114] It is a striking and, I think, productively suggestive fact that references to the Fourth Gospel are relatively numerous in the massive book on the theology and history of Jewish Christianity by H.-J. Schoeps; yet the question we are investigating is not posed there.

[115] See notes 111 and 112 above.

## C. The Scenes in R 1, 62-68
## and the Gospel of John

We come then finally to the key passages which lie between
R 1, 62 and R 1, 68 and which would seem to reflect motifs of
persecution comparable to some in the Fourth Gospel. Here we
have no guidance from previous interpreters. Even though a
number of them have been particularly concerned with the question of possible dependence on John, none have sensed any
marks of dependence in this material. It is relatively easy, therefore, to allow the analysis to proceed in an even-handed manner.
Six passages demand our careful attention:

### R 1, 62, 1

Interpreters who have analyzed the role of Scripture in the
Pseudo-Clementines have regularly noted the presence of passages which show dependence upon conflated texts and/or allusions, a phenomenon common, in fact, in the New Testament
itself, in rabbinic literature, and in the writings of the Church
Fathers.[116] For our Jewish-Christian author, as for many rabbis
and theologians, to think of one text is to have another called to
mind, so that the two blend into a "combined text."

A clear example lies before us in R 1, 41. The author speaks
of Jesus as the Mosaic prophet who,

. . . although he cured every sickness and infirmity among
the people, worked innumerable miracles, and preached eter-

---

[116]The analysis of the role of Scripture made by Waitz in *Pseudo
klementinen* remains the most comprehensive; the corresponding treatment in Strecker's *Judenchristentum* is far less extensive but generally
more trustworthy. Waitz's conclusion that his investigation of the
Scripture citations strongly confirmed his source analysis is largely denied by Strecker (p. 136). The conclusions of the present article lend
some support to Waitz, though in a way which is rather differently
nuanced.

nal life, was rushed to the cross by wicked men. This deed was, however, turned to good by his power.

Thus far the author is clearly drawing upon elements of the so-called "Jesus kerygma" in Acts (e.g., 2:22-24; 3:13-15; 4:10; 5:30; 13:29-32). He continues by turning to the Gospels of Luke and Matthew:

> In short, while he was suffering, all the world suffered with him; for the sun was darkened (Lk. 23:45), the mountains were torn apart, the graves were opened (Mt. 27:51b and c), the veil of the temple was rent (Mt. 27:51a and parallels). . . .

It belongs to the nature of a mixed text, of course, that it is created by addition. Hence, to say the obvious, if, in the present case, the elements drawn from Acts be subtracted, what remains is evidence of indebtedness to Luke and Matthew. Our question now becomes whether a similar phenomenon lies before us in R 1, 62, 1.

Here again we see the author employing a New Testament text, Acts 4. Allowing Caiaphas to stand in the place of the Sanhedrin (Acts 4:5f. mentions Caiaphas together with rulers, elders, scribes, Annas, John, Alexander, and all of the high-priestly family), he draws two motifs from the trial scene:

| *R 1, 62, 1* | *Acts 4:6, 17, 18, 21, 29* |
|---|---|
| Then Caiaphas, again looking at me, sometimes in the way of *warning* and sometimes in that of accusation, said that *I ought for the future to cease preaching Christ Jesus*, | . . . Caiaphas . . . in order that it may spread no further among the people, let us *warn* them . . . so they called them and charged them *not to speak or teach at all in the name of Jesus* . . . and when they had further threatened them. . . . |

*John 16:2; 7:12, 47*

| | |
|---|---|
| lest I should cause *the de-struction of my life*, by being led astray after him (Christ) and by *leading others astray* [partly Syriac].[117] | . . . whoever *kills you* will think he is offering service to God. . . . He is *leading the people astray*. |

The author's dependence on Acts is plain to see. From Acts 4:6, 17, 18, 21, 29 he has taken the picture of a Jewish authority, Caiaphas, warning a Jewish Christian, Peter, to cease preaching Christ Jesus. One notes also that when the Acts material is subtracted, three motifs remain: (1) For Peter to continue to preach Jesus Christ among his Jewish brethren would very likely lead to his death, not only because (2) he would show in this manner that he himself had been led astray, but also because (3) he would be leading others astray. Can we locate the origin of these additional motifs?

Perhaps the author himself conceived them, simply developing them out of the threatening atmosphere of the trial scene in Acts 4. One will want to note, however, another possibility. Rufinus rendered the (lost) Greek text by twice employing the expression *errore decipio*, which need mean nothing more specific than to deceive: " . . . being deceived myself, I should also deceive others." We are at a juncture at which it is profitable to compare Rufinus' Latin translation with the Syriac text, for after doing so we are led to conclude that this is one of those numerous instances in which Rufinus elected a somewhat general manner of expression where the original text was more specific. The key word in the Syriac is ṭ' ', which Frankenburg correctly rendered by the Greek verb *planan*.[118] Both of these terms *may* have the general force of "deceiving another person," but they also carry the specific denotation of "leading another person astray into

---

[117]The Latin and Syriac texts are discussed below.

[118]Frankenburg, *Die syrischen Clementinen mit griechischen Paralleltext* (Berlin, 1937), *ad loc.*

false belief." It is this specific denotation which best fits the context in R 1, 62, 1. Indeed Caiaphas' warning to Peter may very well stand on a well-defined point of Jewish law: those who lead others astray in a matter of idolatry are legally subject to execution as theological seducers (*Messithim*; *planoi*). The legal details are discussed in Mishna Sanhedrin 7, 10, the case of the seducer (*Messith*).[119]

Returning to the New Testament, one observes that the key term *planan* (to lead astray) emerges in John 7:12 and 47, and that at these two points the Peshitta renders by means of t' '. Beyond these verbal observations one notes also that the specific legal denotation of these terms—absent from Acts 4 and 5—seems to be clearly reflected in the New Testament nowhere except in the Fourth Gospel, where the prediction of the martyrdom of Jewish Christians at the hands of Jewish authorities (John 16:2) may be related to the charge that the former are deceived preachers who lead others astray into false worship (Jn. 7:12, 47; cf. 5:18).[120] Comparison of R 1, 62, 1b with these Johannine texts does not lead one to posit literary dependence. Some kind of relationship, however, would seem rather probable.

### R 1, 62, 2

The passage continues immediately, via an adverbial expression.

| *R 1, 62, 2* | *Acts 4:13* |
|---|---|
| Then, moreover, he charged me with *presumption*, because, although I was *unlearned*, a fisherman and a *rustic*, | . . . and perceiving that they were *uneducated and common men*, they were amazed. . . . |

---

[119] See also Martyn, *History and Theology in the Fourth Gospel*, final pages of chapter 3, and Excursus C, not least the comments about the verb t'h.

[120] *Ibid.*

|  | *John 9:34* |
|---|---|
| *I dared to assume the office of a teacher.* | You were *born in utter sin*, and *would you teach us?* |

The author's dependence on Acts is clear, and again when the marks of his indebtedness to Acts are subtracted, a quite distinct motif remains, that of an authoritative Jewish questioner accusing a Jewish Christian of showing temerity, since, being himself unlearned, he has dared to assume the office of a teacher. Where did the author get this motif?

Not from Acts 4. In that text the learned are *amazed* (cf. Mk. 1:22 and Jn. 7:15) at the *boldness* of the unlearned, not *offended* at their *presumption* to be teachers. In another trial scene, however, the one in John 9, the climax is provided in part by precisely this motif, as the text above shows. There the authoritative examiners excoriate the formerly blind man for his temerity in presuming to teach them.

To be sure, one might also think of such texts as Mark 1:22, Luke 2:46f., and Matthew 13:54ff. (cf. John 7:15), but these contain only the motifs of a man teaching, even though he lacks formal training, and of others experiencing amazement at his activity. The added note provided in the charge of temerity and presumptuousness is, within the New Testament, peculiar to John 9:34.

Do we have, then, a mixed text, created by our author's drawing literarily on both Acts 4 and John 9? This is perhaps possible, but by no means does the evidence require it. One may in fact note literarily a contrast between R 1, 62, 2 and R 2, 48. The latter passage evidences a clear example of a mixed text, consisting of Matthew 11:27 plus John 1:1 and 5:23. As regards R 1, 62, 2, however, it will be wise, at least for the moment, to speak of a conflation which brings together elements drawn from Acts and a motif, which is, within the New Testament, peculiar to John.

## R 1, 62, 5

In this passage one would not speak, I think, of a strong case for conflation, but in the context of the other passages it is sufficiently pertinent to be displayed.

| *R 1, 62, 5* | *Acts 4:13* |
|---|---|
| [Peter remarks to the authoritative Caiaphas:] . . . if I, an *unlearned and uneducated man*, as you say, a fisherman and a rustic, | . . . and perceiving that they were *uneducated and common men* they were amazed. . . . |
| | *John 9:30-33* |
| | [The formerly blind man remarks to the examining authorities:] The amazing thing is that *you do not know* where he (Jesus) comes from; *yet he opened my eyes*. . . . |
| *have more understanding than wise elders*, this, I said, ought the more to strike terror into you. | |

Here again there is the element drawn from Acts 4:13, and one notes the possibility of a significant parallel with John 9:30-33.

## R 1, 65, 1-3

R 1, 65-68 is not actually a literary sub-unit. The sub-unit begins at 1, 66 as a number of commentators have noted (Rehm places the paragraph at 1, 66, 2). But a consideration of the dramatis personae shows that 1, 66-71 is tied to the preceding in part by the introduction in 1, 65 of a new character who remains on stage, so to speak, into 1, 68. The character is Gamaliel, a figure our author has clearly drawn from Acts (he is mentioned only twice in the New Testament: Acts 5:34ff. and Acts 22:3). Note how he paints Gamaliel's picture: he has Gamaliel make two speeches, the last of the speeches made on day number one, and the first of those made on day number two. The former of these (1, 65) is occasioned by an uproar among the priests, which uproar had been caused, in turn, by Peter's prophecy that failure to terminate the sacrificial system would bring about the destruction of the temple. At the uproar, Gamaliel rises and restores order by a relatively brief speech.

*R 1, 65, 1-3*

*When I (Peter) had thus spoken*, the whole multitude of the priests were in a *rage*, because I had foretold the overthrow of the temple. When *Gamaliel, a chief of the people*, saw it—*who was secretly our brother in the faith*, but by our advice *remained among them*— . . . he *stood up and said*, "Be quiet for a little while, O *men of Israel*, for you do not perceive the trial which hangs over you. Wherefore, *refrain from these men. If what they are engaged in is of human counsel, it will soon come to an end; but if it is from God*, why will *you* sin without cause and *gain nothing? For who can overpower the will of God?* . . ."

*Acts 5:33-35, 38, 39*

*When they heard this*, they were

*enraged* and wanted to kill them. But a Pharisee *in the council* named Gamaliel, a teacher of the law *held in honor by all the people*,

*stood up and said to them*, "Men of Israel, take care what you do with these men. . . . *Keep away from these men and let them alone. For if this plan or this undertaking be of men, it will fail; but if it is of God, you will not be able to overthrow them, lest you be found opposing God."*

*John    3:1;    7:50-52;    12:42;*
*19:38-40*

Now there was a man of the Pharisees named Nicodemus, *a ruler of the Jews.* . . . Nicodemus, who had gone to him before, and who was one of them, said to them, "Does our Law judge a man without first giving him a hearing . . .?" They replied, "Are you from Galilee too?" . . . Many even of the *rulers believed in him* but for fear of the Pharisees they *did not confess it.* . . . After this Joseph of Arimathea came and took

> away his body. Nicodemus also . . . came. . . . They took the body of Jesus. . . .

Beyond what is set out in this exhibit, Gamaliel continues by promising himself to dispute with the Jewish Christians on the following day, and his speech partially calms the priests, who apparently anticipate that on the morrow Gamaliel will publicly convict the Christians of error (the reader of the *Ascents* knows, of course, that Gamaliel is a secret Christian who will do no such thing).

For the part of Gamaliel's first speech, exhibited above, approximately two-thirds of the whole, the author clearly drew upon Acts 5:33-35, 38-39. Indeed, the double conditional sentence so closely parallels the one in Acts 5:38-39, as to cause commentators to cite this passage as proof that our author is *literarily dependent on Acts.*

Preceding the speech, however, are two elements which call for separate comment, as possible "leftovers" vis-à-vis Acts 5. The *first, princeps populi* (a ruler of the people), may reflect Gamaliel's identification in Acts 5:34 as "a member of the Sanhedrin . . . a teacher of the Law, held in honor by all the people." One must ask more precisely, however, what Greek words our Jewish-Christian author is likely to have used here. To judge from Rufinus' text, we may doubt that he followed closely Acts 5:34, for in that case we should have expected Rufinus to render the Greek text by some such expression as *legisdoctor honorabilis universae plebi* (a teacher of the Law, held in honor by all the people). Moving the other way, that is, from Rufinus' translation to the Greek, one gets "a ruler of the people," an expression absent from the identification of Gamaliel in Acts 5 (cf. Acts 4:8). In a moment we shall inquire as to the possible origin of this expression.

The *second* leftover element is the pair of clauses enclosed by dashes: Gamaliel is secretly a Christian, but, on the advice of the apostles (or the whole Church), he remains among the non-Christian Jews. Where did our author find this motif?

A number of scholars speak of the present passage as the earliest indication of the legend that Gamaliel was a secret Christian.[121] That may be so, but—as in previous instances—one must still ask whether our author created a new motif, or whether he combined a New Testament text (Acts 5) with a motif reflected elsewhere in the New Testament.

Recalling the figure of Nicodemus in the Fourth Gospel may serve to suggest an affirmative answer, for both of the leftover elements find their best parallels in the Fourth Evangelist's portrait of Nicodemus. He is explicitly identified as a ruler of the Jews, and while the Fourth Evangelist's interpretative intentions as regards Nicodemus' full Christian allegiance may be debated, I believe it is at least clear that he intends to include Nicodemus among the secret believers to whom he refers in 12:42.[122]

It follows that the personage who emerges in R 1, 65 has probably been created by conflating the figure of Gamaliel (peculiar to Acts) with the figure of Nicodemus (peculiar to the Fourth Gospel), or with the equivalent of this latter figure. One may say that this particular conflation did not require an enormous amount of imagination, for in several respects the figures are remarkably similar: both Galamiel and Nicodemus are Pharisees; both are members of the Sanhedrin; and both function in ways advantageous to Jewish Christians who are confronted by hostile Jewish authorities. Indeed, the conflation of Gamaliel and Nicodemus is also attested in the *Acts of Pilate*. I shall return to that fact presently. For the moment the major point is the high degree of probability which attaches to the hypothesis of conflation in R 1, 65, 1-3.

---

[121] Schoeps, *Theologie und Geschichte*, p. 405; references to Schürer and Zahn are accurately given there.

[122] One recalls that the evangelist has Nicodemus accompany and assist the Synoptic Joseph of Arimathea in the sensitively executed task of burying Jesus (Jn. 19:38ff.); and one should note particularly the motif in 19:38—"but secretly for fear of the Jews"—a motif which would seem to suggest that neither Joseph nor Nicodemus is truly a Jew.

## R 1, 67, 1 and R 1, 68, 1

The story of the first day of the disputation ends with R 1, 65. The apostles and their brethren prepare themselves for the second day by visiting "our James," and by praying through the night. In the morning, accompanied by James, they go up once more to the temple, where Gamaliel, the secret believer, resumes his clever and reasonable attempt to gain for the apostles a safe and effective hearing before both Caiaphas and the people as a whole.

| *R 1, 67, 1* | *John 3:1ff.; 7:15, 50f. (cf. 9:34)* |
|---|---|
| If I, Gamaliel, deem it no reproach either to my learning or to my old age to learn something from young and unlearned men . . . ought not this to be the object of love and desire of all, to learn what they do not know, and to teach what they have learned? | (The texts are given in the discussion.) |

(1) The motif of Gamaliel's willingness to be taught by those who are young and unlearned is a relatively easy extension from the portrait in Acts, but, in any case, it is precisely that, a new extension. And, again, it is a motif which in the Fourth Gospel is embodied by Nicodemus. It is this man who, although a ruler of the Jews and a teacher of Israel, comes by night (Jn. 3:1ff.) to receive instruction from a man who never studied (Jn. 7:15). (2) Moreover it is this same Nicodemus who later argues that the council itself should learn from this untutored man exactly what he has done (Jn. 7:50f.). In R 1, 67, 1 these are precisely the two motifs which our Jewish-Christian author has added to the portrait of Gamaliel drawn from Acts.

It should also be noted—as in R 1, 62, 1 above—that the

Caiaphas of the *Ascents* is presented in terms which cause him to look somewhat like the colleagues of Nicodemus in the Fourth Gospel. The latter refuse Nicodemus' plea to learn from the accused (7:52); and their equivalents in John 9, those who examine the blind man, make the same refusal: "You were born in utter sin, and will you teach us?"

|  *R 1, 68, 1*  |  *John 7:50-52*  |
|---|---|
| These sayings of Gamaliel did not much please Caiaphas; and holding him in suspicion, as it seemed . . . | Nicodemus said to them. . . . They replied, "Are you from Galilee too?" |

The speech of Gamaliel in Acts 5 is considered by his colleagues to be an eminently reasonable utterance. Far from holding him in suspicion, they accept his advice and act on it. The major motif of R 1, 68, 1 is clearly not drawn, then, from Acts. It finds its parallel, rather, in John 7:52. Here Nicodemus' speech to his colleagues-in-council does arouse their suspicions that he may have succumbed to the Christian message. Thus we see another datum which indicates that our Jewish-Christian author has conflated the Acts portrait of Gamaliel with motifs which in the New Testament attach only to the Johannine portrait of Nicodemus.

\*       \*       \*

It is now time for us to gather up the loose ends in order to see what we may have before us as a whole.

1. Whereas there is clear evidence that our second-century, Jewish-Christian author drew direct quotations from Acts and from the Synoptic Gospels, there is not a single convincing case for a *quotation* from the Fourth Gospel.

2. The initial phase of our study of possible Johannine *allusions* produced results which are harmonious with the absence of quotations from John. Indeed, even where the subject matter would lead one to expect such allusions, they prove to be absent. Were one to judge on the basis of the data to this point—roughly

speaking, the data forthcoming from the research of previous scholars—he would be compelled to conclude either that the author was ignorant of the Fourth Gospel (as Waitz thought) or that he had a relationship to it so different from that which he had to the Synoptics as to cause him to give absolutely no indication of his knowledge of it.

3. Is this picture altered by the additional data we have studied in the passages from R 1, 62 to R 1, 68? For a moment one might consider the possibility, I suppose, that these data merely reflect the accidental emergence of similar motifs. For two major reasons, however, I should consider it quite probable that we are dealing with parallels which have arisen because of some kind of specific connection.

First, all six of them are found in a relatively short compass, rather than scattered here and there. They are primarily focused on only two figures: Peter—a Jewish Christian who dares to carry on a mission among his Jewish brethren—and Gamaliel—a member of the council who is secretly a Jewish Christian. They begin as soon as Peter takes up his direct speech, they emerge next in connection with Gamaliel, and they cease when Gamaliel steps off the stage. Thus the parallels do not constitute disparate snippets which might present accidental similarities.

Second, as I have already briefly noted, the conflation of the figures of Gamaliel and Nicodemus is evidenced elsehwere, and, in fact, is a work—the *Acts of Pilate*—which probably stems from the pen of a Jewish Christian of the same general period.[123] That fact encourages one to think that our author's portrait of Gamaliel does not possess features similar to those of Nicodemus simply by chance.

In short, then, the added data in R 1, 62, 65, 67, and 68 do indeed alter the picture. Taking them into account *requires* an explanation of the text of the *Ascents* which somehow involves the Fourth Gospel. Exactly how the Fourth Gospel is involved is a question which could lead to either of two hypotheses.

---

[123] See F. Scheidweiler, "The Gospel of Nicodemus, Acts of Pilate and Christ's descent into Hell," Hennecke-Schneemelcher, *New Testament Apocrypha* I, 444ff.

## IV. Two Hypotheses

There are two major possibilities: A. Since the added data do not indicate a direct literary relationship, the most one may claim is that the author had at some time read the Fourth Gospel, and that he was therefore able to recall at least some of its motifs by memory:

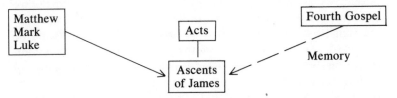

B. The data are also susceptible to explanation on the assumption that there was no link at all leading from the Fourth Gospel to the *Ascents*. In this case, one would be speaking of traditional elements which made their way along two independent routes both to the Fourth Gospel and to the *Ascents*:

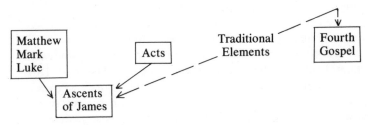

We may make our way forward by exploring the two hypotheses in the light of the Jewish-Christian identity of the author of the *Ascents*.

### A. A memory link from the Fourth Gospel to the *Ascents of James*

This is an attractive hypothesis on several counts:
1. We know that when R. E. Brown has called "a recasting and joining of canonical materials" is the key to the composition

of two second-century works: Tatian's *Diatessaron* (Rome ca. 175 A.D.?) and the Papyrus Egerton 2 (Egypt ca. 150 A.D.?); and the composition of each of these involved use of the Fourth Gospel.[124] Neither is the work of a Jewish Christian, and that fact must be borne in mind, but they do provide examples of a literary process *somewhat* similar to that posited by this first hypothesis.

2. The acceptance of this hypothesis would ease one of the difficulties we have observed earlier. At several junctures, we have had occasion to note that the *Ascents* seems to give conflicting signals: no use of the Fourth Gospel where such would be expected, several indications of its possible use in a context dominated by its indebtedness to Acts. These signals are perhaps not unduly puzzling on the hypothesis of a memory link, for memory is always selective. One could imagine that from the author's reading of the Fourth Gospel he recalled the figure of Nicodemus, but did not remember Jesus' conversation with the Samaritan woman, etc. Just why a Jewish Christian would remember and forget in the required pattern might be a question difficult or impossible to answer, but early Christian literature has bequeathed to us a host of such questions.

3. Returning to the specific phenomenon of the "doubling" of Gamaliel and Nicodemus, one may note that as a technique, doubling is quite common in early Christian literature, not least in the later layers of the Pseudo-Clementines themselves. To be sure, the specific parallel which is, as I mentioned above, so carefully developed in the *Acts of Pilate*, rests on a direct, *literary* borrowing from both Acts and the Fourth Gospel. A memory link as regards the figure of Nicodemus is, however, perfectly adequate to explain the pertinent data in the *Ascents*.

4. Moreover, a memory link as opposed to direct literary dependence could be seen as quite harmonious with the author's identity as a Jewish Christian. One recalls the presence in the Fourth Gospel of sharp polemic probably directed against Jewish Christians (e.g., John 8:31ff.).[125] On the assumption of such

---

[124]R. E. Brown, "The Relation of 'The Secret Gospel of Mark' to the Fourth Gospel," *CBQ* 36 (1974; Skehan Festschrift) 466-485 (477).

[125]See the section on John 8:31ff. in Chapter 3 of the present volume.

polemic, it is not overly difficult to imagine that this Gospel would constitute a special category in the mind of a Jewish-Christian author. If he allowed his memory to draw on it at all, he would surely do so in such a way as to pick the flowers from among the thorns.

In short, the data we have encountered in the disputation of R 1, 62ff. may open up to us a small part of a hitherto unattended chapter in the history of the interpretation of John, the chapter, namely, which deals with the Gospel's interpretation among Jewish Christians. As far as I can see, the possibility of such a chapter is hinted at neither by the scholars expert in the history of Johannine interpretation—from Loewenich to Pagels[126]—nor by those who specialize in the study of Jewish Christianity.[127]

To be sure, the pertinent data in the *Ascents* are neither numerous nor extensive. On the hypothesis of a memory link, one would say that they suffice only to indicate (a) that the (offensive?) Fourth Gospel had no honored place alongside the other Gospels in the literary treasury of the second-century church of Pella, but (b) that at least one member of that church—a writer of some talent—had read it and was willing to draw a few motifs from it by memory.

By the same token, however, mentioning a Jewish-Christian chapter in the history of the interpretation of John may lead one at least to ask whether an exploration of the recoverable attitudes of Jewish Christians toward the Fourth Gospel would, after all, provide support for the hypothesis of a memory link. There are good grounds for holding that our author lived in a Jewish-Christian community which had not been penetrated by Gnostic forms of thought.[128] A brief survey of the literature useful for the study of Jewish Christianity yields the hint that, while the Fourth Gospel was occasionally used among Gnosticizing Jewish Christians—e.g., those of the *Kerygmata Petrou*[129]—it may have

---

[126] See note 91 above.

[127] See the pertinent works of, among others, H.-J. Schoeps, J. Daniélou, M. Simon, G. Strecker, B. Bagatti, and E. Testa. Cf. also the Daniélou Festschrift mentioned in note 5 above.

[128] Strecker, *Judenchristentum*, p. 254 n.

[129] *Ibid.*, p. 218.

been mostly avoided in communities like that of our author.[130]
Even if this hint should prove correct, it would not exclude, of
course, a memory link on the part of one member of such a
community. Hence, I should be far from setting aside this first
hypothesis. I say only that a cursory survey hints that the presence in the Fourth Gospel of polemic against Jewish Christians
may in fact have caused that Gospel to be studiously avoided by
Jewish Christians who lacked the connecting bridge of Gnostic
thought-forms. In any case, one should at least consider seriously
the second alternative.

### B. Traditional elements held in common
### by the authors of the Fourth Gospel
### and of the *Ascents of James*

There are several reasons to think that the parallels reflect
not a link with the Fourth Gospel itself—even by memory—but
rather the effects on the two documents of traditional elements
antedating both of them.

1. This hypothesis avoids altogether the difficulty of holding
that our Jewish-Christian author was willing to borrow from that
Gospel in which "the Jews who had believed in him" are characterized as having the devil as their father (Jn. 8:31, 44). Nor

---

[130]There is a fascinating and, as far as I can see, largely overlooked
passage in Epiphanius, *Panarion* (30, 3, 8) which *could* be cited, I suppose, to indicate use of the Fourth Gospel by Jewish Christians. It comes
in the discussion of the Ebionites. After saying that the latter accept and
use only the Gospel of Matthew, Epiphanius mentions that some Jewish
Christians have transmitted the following information: The Gospel of
John, translated from Greek into Hebrew, has been secretly stored in
some Jewish genizahs in Tiberias. This is the sort of datum which makes
one's head reel a bit, not only because it is so astonishing, but also
because the interpretative possibilities are so numerous. In the present
note there is sufficient space only to say that after pondering the text
itself in its context, and after consulting the corresponding texts (a) of the
pertinent anakephalaiosis (summary) in the *Panarion* (*GCS* 25, 236) and
(b) of *Anakephalaiosis* 30 (*PG* 42, 857), I see no grounds for drawing from
*Panarion* 30, 3, 8 the conclusion that the Fourth Gospel was read and
interpreted by non-Gnosticizing Jewish Christians.

should one think it truly strange that an author of the second half of the second century—especially a Jewish-Christian author— should be ignorant of the Fourth Gospel or should consciously avoid it. Nothing requires us to date the *Ascents* any appreciable distances at all from Justin, and while the apologist *may* have drawn on the Fourth Gospel, to a number of interpreters it seems far more likely that he did not do so.[131] It is now clear that well into the second century one or more of the written Gospels often circulated in the company of Gospel traditions in oral form.[132] Moreover, we may have evidence of such parallel circulation of written and oral Gospel materials in the *Ascents* itself. A comparison of R 1, 37 and R 1, 39 with Luke 21:20ff. may tell us that the Pella legend made its way along two independent routes, to Luke on the one hand, and to our author on the other. What we have called "Johannine motifs" in R 1, 62-68 could very well constitute an analogous case.

2. There is no instance of a verbal agreement extending beyond one or two words. This may be credited, of course, to a memory link, but it is perhaps a bit more readily explained as the result of a shared tradition. Repeatedly, when we subtracted the influence of Acts, what remained was made up, not of Johannine sentences, or even clauses, but rather of motifs which are paralleled in John.

3. Moreover—and this is, I believe, a weighty observation—these motifs all have a common *Sitz im Leben* (life situation). One notices that the pertinent data in the Fourth Gospel fall, without significant exception, in the first verses of Chapter 16 and in the latter parts of Chapters 7 and 9—that is to say, in texts which reflect the situation of a Jewish Christian being subjected to a hearing or trial before a Jewish court (a *Bet Din*; John 3:1; 7:12; 15 preserve supplementary notes).[133] From the Synoptic tradition we know that early Jewish Christians were re-

---

[131] See, e.g., the discussions in the commentaries by Barrett (pp. 93ff.) and Schnackenburg (ET 1, 199) and in Braun, *Jean le Théologien*, pp. 135ff., 290f.

[132] Cf. H. Köster, *Synoptische Überlieferung bei den Apostolischen Vätern* (Berlin, 1957); A. J. Bellinzoni, *The Sayings of Jesus.*

[133] See Martyn, *History and Theology*, Chapter 3.

peatedly brought before Jewish courts (Mk. 13:9a; Mt. 10:17; Lk. 12:11; 21:12a), so that it is technically proper to speak of that setting as a *Sitz im Leben*, and it is that single *Sitz im Leben* which lies behind all the Johannine data to which we have been led. To be sure, the scene in the *Ascents* is that of a public disputation to which the Jewish Christians have been invited, however urgently. For a talented author, however, such a scene is not far removed from the *Sitz im Leben* of a legal hearing.

In short, the hypothesis of shared elements of tradition does not require us to think of six disparate elements making their way along as many independent routes both to the fourth evangelist and to our Jewish-Christian author. One has only to imagine that both of these authors received what would be essentially a single piece of tradition, and this point proves, in fact, to be a distinct strength of our second hypothesis. If the author of the *Ascents* inherited a unified piece of tradition pertaining to the *Sitz im Leben* of a trial before a Jewish court—and this is all that is required by the data—it is not at all puzzling that he should compose the Samaritan debate and other pieces without reflecting in any way a knowledge of the Fourth Gospel. The hypothetical piece of tradition would amount to something like the following:

A Jewish Christian is on trial before a Bet Din on the capital charge of having led astray some of his fellow Jews;[a] in this setting, aware of the illumination of the Gospel, he offers instruction to his judges,[b] who, with one exception, refuse to be taught by an unlettered man, charging him with temerity;[c] the exception is a council member who secretly harbors pro-Christian sentiments;[d] he guardedly expresses these sentiments by suggesting that the court listen to the testimony of the accused,[e] and this move earns for him the suspicion of his colleagues.[f]

[a] John 16:2; 7:12, 47 (cf. Mark 13:9a); R 1, 62, 1
[b] John 9:30-33 (cf. Mark 13:9b); R 1, 62, 5
[c] John 7:52; 9:34; R 1, 62, 2; 1, 67, 1
[d] John 7:50ff.; 12:42; 3:1; R 1, 65, 1-3
[e] John 7:51; R 1, 67, 1
[f] John 7:52; R 1, 68, 1

In light of this hypothesis, we must alter in important ways the diagram used earlier to illustrate our second hypothesis:

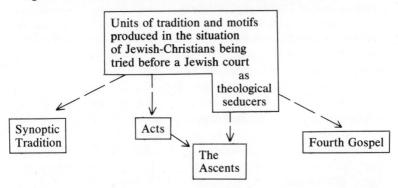

*Ex hypothesi*—let this expression be understood from this point forward, so as to avoid the cumbersome use of the English subjunctive—there is good reason to believe that this piece of tradition—*in the form involving the seducer charge*—was fixed in or quite near the setting in which the Fourth Gospel was written; and it would follow that the tradition probably reflected actual developments which had transpired in the life of John's own community.[134] The portrait of a secret believer among the synagogue rulers, for example, would probably not be *at this stage* (cf. Jn. 12:42) merely a "literary motif,"[135] although there can be little doubt that, along with other elements, it later became exactly that (*Acts of Pilate*). On the contrary, in its Johannine

---

[134]Martyn, *History and Theology*, Chapter 3.

[135]Contra Strecker, *Judenchristentum*, p. 253. The careful reader of Strecker's monograph senses that between the lines the author is carrying on a polemic against the historical credulity of H.-J. Schoeps. As regards this particular form of the historicity debate, I find myself in agreement, for the most part, with Strecker, as the following paragraph in the text above will show. If, in interpreting the *Ascents*, someone uses the adjective "historical" to claim that the document puts us in touch with specific events essentially like those which it purports to describe—largely the opinion of Schoeps—I should much prefer Strecker's repeated emphasis on "literary motifs." On the other hand, the adjective "historical" may also be justly used in a broader way to refer to a repeated *Sitz im Leben*, and this use is what seems called for by the Johannine parallels.

form the unit of tradition would have represented an historical specification of the Synoptic loging about Christians being brought before synagogue councils.

Its use by the author of the *Ascents*, on the other hand, shows that for him (and his community) it had become nothing other than a piece of tradition, available to this *littérateur* who wished to employ it for the sake of its literary potential. This can be seen already from the fact that the author employed it, not in the *Sitz im Leben* (repeated situation) of a trial before a Jewish court, but rather in an imaginary, "once-upon-a-time" disputation, in which the Jewish-Christian disputants of the Jerusalem church are presented as having been dramatically victorious over the chief priest himself. One notes also that the author rationalized a number of the tradition's motifs, virtually changing them into timeless aphorisms:

> . . . ought not this to be the . . . desire of all, to learn what they do not know? . . . For it is certain that neither friendship, nor kindred, nor lofty power, ought to be more precious to men than truth (R 1, 67, 1-2).

Finally, in reaching these conclusions, we must avoid two errors. From the hypothesis it follows clearly that we must not allow the author's literary gifts and his rationalistic tendencies to cause us to suppose that he created the disputation on the dual basis of the canonical Acts and his own imagination, thus fashioning nothing other than literary motifs. On the contrary, his fertile imagination seems clearly to have enjoyed the stimulus not only of Acts, but also of the piece of tradition we have hypothetically isolated. At the same time, we must not allow the author's dramatic gifts to cause us to think that he preserved accurate information about a disputation which actually transpired in the early days of the Jerusalem church. He is a talented *littérateur* who believes that his own Jewish-Christian church, far removed from the early days in Jerusalem and living even at considerable distance from persecution at the hands of Jewish courts, needs once again to learn of its identity in distinction both from the identity of its parent—non-Christian Judaism—and from that of its illegitimate sibling—Pauline Christianity. On the basis of our second hypothesis, one would say that for presenting the former of these two distinctions our author had at his disposal, among other materials, a piece of Jewish-Christian tradition which found its essential form at a time in the life of the community behind the Fourth Gospel when that community was a Jewish-Christian church.

# CHAPTER 3

# Glimpses into the History
# of the Johannine Community

**From Its Origin Through the Period of Its Life in Which
the Fourth Gospel Was Composed**

## INTRODUCTION

In composing the present chapter, I have taken for granted a few presuppositions which ought to be made clear at the outset:

1. In three respects the Fourth Gospel is comparable to what archaeologists call a "tell." (a) First, there are numerous literary strata, and to some extent these strata may be differentiated from one another.[136] (b) Second, much of the substance of the "materials" in the strata is of such a character as to reflect communal interests, concerns, and experiences.[137] (c) Third, considered as a whole, this literary "tell" exhibits a remarkable degree of stylis-

---

[136]See, e.g., the analysis proposed by R. E. Brown, John (I-XII), pp. xxxiv-xl. The major criterion for strata differentiation is the aporia. See note 138 below.

[137]This point has been grasped by many interpreters. See Martyn, *History and Theology*, p. xviii and *passim*; David E. Aune, *The Cultic Setting of Realized Eschatology in Early Christianity* (Leiden, 1972), pp. 73-84.

tic and conceptual homogeneity.[138] Now, taking into account all three of these observations, one sees that we are dealing with a stratified literary deposit from what archaeologists would call a single, continuous occupation. In other words, the literary history behind the Fourth Gospel reflects to a large degree the history of a single community which maintained over a period of some duration its particular and rather peculiar identity. It obviously follows that we may hope to draw from the *Gospel's literary history* certain conclusions about the *community's social and theological history*. In the present chapter there will not be sufficient space to demonstrate in every case the literary-critical grounds. I can only say that the fundamental attempt is to move from relatively secure points in the document's literary history to reasonable hypotheses as regards the community's social and theological history.

2. A second presupposition is that the Gospel was written for the Johannine community. That is to say, it was written for a community of people who had a shared history and who in the course of that history developed a highly symbolic language with numerous expressions which *they* would easily understand as referring to their shared history. In short, to a large extent the Gospel is written in the language of a community of initiates. It follows that those who would be historians of this community must not only engage in literary archaeology, but must also make at least a partial entry into this symbolic language. That is no small undertaking. On the contrary, it requires all of the scientific control and all of the informed, historical imagination we can corporately muster. The fact that these two gifts are somewhat unevenly distributed among us is one of the reasons we must help one another by mutual enrichment and by mutual correction (Rom. 1:11).

---

[138]E. Ruckstuhl, *Die literarische Einheit*; see also Professor Ruckstuhl's essay in M. de Jonge (ed.), *L'Évangile de Jean*. His critique of the work of R. T. Fortna is careful and weighty. Johannine source critics will have to reckon with Ruckstuhl's renewed challenge as regards the use of stylistic observations. The major criterion for strata differentiation, however, the criterion of the aporiae, remains intact. Cf. Robert Kysar, *The Fourth Evangelist*, Chapter 1.

3. In the course of this chapter it will become apparent that I believe studies in Jewish Christianity hold considerable promise for historians of the Johannine community and for Johannine interpreters in general. There are some new labors in this area, and I think they may be expected to bear some fruit in Johannine studies.[139]

So much for presuppositions. I should also say a brief word about the indicative mood and the subjunctive mood. Considering the widespread use of the indicative mood in the work of historians, it has occurred to me that it would be a valuable practice for the historian to rise each morning saying to himself three times slowly and with emphasis, "I do not know." The direct pertinence of this suggestion to the present chapter will be at least partially grasped if the reader will bear in mind the necessity to interpret a good many of my indicative verbs as though they were in the subjunctive mood. The number of points in the history of the Johannine community about which we may be virtually certain is relatively small, and we need to be clear about that. .

One of these relatively secure points is surely the highly probable correspondence to the *Birkath ha-Minim* (Benediction Against Heretics) of the expressions "to be put out of the synagogue" and "to put someone out of the synagogue" which emerge in John 9:22, 12:42 and 16:2. While concern for clarity has caused me to present the following "glimpses" in chronological order, the perception of them began not with observations and hypotheses pertinent to what I have termed the early period, but rather with this secure point of correspondence.[140] From this point I have tried to work both backward and forward literarily and historically.[141]

---

[139] In addition to the well-known works of Schoeps, Daniélou, Simon *et al.*, see Klijn and Reinink, *Patristic Evidence*. Cf. also Chapters 1 and 2 of the present volume.

[140] See Martyn, *History and Theology, passim.*

[141] See Meeks, *"Am I a Jew?"* In Meeks' generous and helpful appraisal of the essay I contributed to the Pittsburgh Festival of the Gospels (*Jesus and Man's Hope* I, pp. 247-273), he remarks that while my "fascinating proposals" constitute a "prolific working hypothesis . . . the weakest point . . . is just the starting point: the attempt to reconstruct a

# I. THE EARLY PERIOD

*The Conception of a Messianic Group Within
the Community of the Synagogue*

The statement of Martin Dibelius, "In the beginning was the sermon," is not only famous;[142] it has also been enormously influential in New Testament studies. Perhaps, indeed, it is this very statement which lies ultimately behind the wide agreement today that "the Fourth Gospel began life as separate homilies."[143] The question is whether we can determine which of the recoverable homilies are likely to be the earliest.

A strong case may be made, I believe, for holding that a recoverable literary stratum behind 1:35-49 constitutes part of a very early sermon, perhaps indeed one of those evangelistic sermons, which by definition must have lain at the origin of the Johannine community.[144] There are several reasons for holding this opinion:

　　1. Verse 43 contains clear indications of editorial activity on

---

single, unitary *narrative* source independently of form- and redaction-critical study of the *discourse* material" (p. 184). This is a critique of the source-critical labors of Robert Fortna and of my taking those labors as my first hypothesis (Pittsburgh essay, p. 248). At the present juncture three things must be said: (1) I believe Fortna's analysis to be the best and most helpful source criticism of the Fourth Gospel we have to date. (2) Meeks is surely right that Fortna's work must be reviewed on the basis of form- and redaction-critical study of the discourses. This constitutes a *desideratum* in Johannine studies. (3) Actually both in the Pittsburgh essay and in the present one the "starting point" of my analysis, as distinguished from the point at which the presentation of results begins, is John 9:22.

　　[142]Martin Dibelius, *Die alttestamentlichen Motive in der Leidensgeschichte des Petrus- und des Johannes-Evangeliums*, p. 242 of the reprint in *Botschaft und Geschichte* I (Tübingen, 1953).

　　[143]Lindars, *Behind the Fourth Gospel* (London, 1971), p. 47.

　　[144]Verse 49 is fixed as the end of the pericope by the observation that John 1:50 is probably the evangelist's composition, placed as it is to function as a bridge leading from the tradition behind 1:35-49 to the logion of verse 51. As regards beginning the pericope with verse 35 cf. M. de Jonge, "Jesus as Prophet and King in the Fourth Gospel," in *ETL* 49

the part of *someone*. We recall some vexing syntactical problems, discussed at some length in Chapter 1 above.[145] There is moreover a structural problem which is created by verse 43.[146] Elsewhere in this tightly-knit pericope the present tense of the verb "to find" serves as the means by which the witness-chain is continuously extended from John the Baptist outward (vv. 41 and 45; cf. 35ff.). As it stands, verse 43 breaks this chain by allowing Jesus to be the subject of "he found." Several explanations are possible, of course.[147] In my opinion the most probable explanation is to identify the syntactical and structural problems as *aporias* introduced into the text by someone who edited an earlier tradition or source. In its earlier form verse 43 probably mentioned Andrew (or Simon) as the subject of "he found."[148] Thus

---

(1973), p. 163f, where 1:19-34 is correctly identified as a pericope. In the present essay I am using the terms "sermon" and "homily" to refer to messages actually preached in the Johannine group/community. I do not intend to imply that the very words of the recoverable literary stratum behind John 1:35-49 constituted such a message, but rather that they *encapsulate part* of an early sermon. At a later point I shall make a similar suggestion about John 8:31ff. These suggestions are also to be distinguished from the claim that we have before us an example representative of a form-critical category which can be identified as a "homily." See the trenchant observations made on this subject by K. P. Donfried, *The Setting of Second Clement in Early Christianity* (Leiden, 1974), pp. 25-34.

[145] The syntactical problems are also discussed in R. E. Brown, *John, ad loc.*; it is one of the disappointing features of the generally helpful commentary by Barnabas Lindars that *problems* posed by the text are not infrequently smoothed over, rather than wrestled with. Lindars' comment on 1:43 is typical of such treatment: "But awkward as it is the text can stand . . . the verse is only aimed at bringing Philip on to the stage, because of his part in what follows."

[146] The structural imbalance was seen and clearly stated by M.-E. Boismard, "Les traditions johanniques concernant le Baptiste", in *RB* 70 (1963) 5-42 (especially p. 40).

[147] F. Spitta, W. Wilkens, and M.-E. Boismard allotted verse 43 to the hand of a post-Johannine redactor. The references to Spitta and Wilkens are given by Boismard on p. 42 of the article cited above in note 146.

[148] See R. E. Brown, *John, ad loc.*, and Chapter 1 of the present volume.

the pericope originally portrayed Jesus in a remarkably passive role. He does not take the major initiative to call disciples. On the contrary, it is the others who *find* him.

2. With this observation it is harmonious that alongside the striking use of "to find" the verb "to come" emerges in pregnant expressions:

> come and see (v. 39),
> come and see (v. 46),
> to come to Jesus (equivalent expressions in vv. 39, 46, and 47).

Aside from the Baptist, all of the characters in the underlying tradition *come to Jesus* and thereby become his disciples.

3. The roles given to "to find" and "to come" and the concomitant passivity of Jesus constitute an *aporia* when compared with key passages in the Fourth Gospel in which the initiative of Jesus (or of God) is polemically affirmed. Two are particularly striking:[149]

> 6:44 (cf. also 6:65)
>> No one can come to me
>> unless the Father . . . draws him. . . .
> 15:16 (cf. also 15:19)
>> You did not choose me,
>> but I chose you.

The "someone" who edited the earlier tradition or source behind 1:35-49 was very probably the fourth evangelist himself. Part of his motivation for altering verse 43 presumably lay in the desire to show Jesus taking the initiative in this instance (cf. also v. 48c).

4. The roles given to "to find" and "to come" also differentiate the underlying tradition rather sharply from the Synoptic pericopes commonly referred to as "The *Call* of the Disciples."[150]

---

[149] Cf. also Jn. 5:14 and 9:35.

[150] For a discussion of Hahn's analysis of this pericope see note 65.

In the latter, as the name correctly implies, Jesus consistently takes the entire initiative to call disciples. In the tradition underlying John 1:35-49, to the contrary, we have already noted that Jesus is dominantly presented as a passive figure who is successively *found* by men who *come to him*.

From these four observations it follows with some degree of probability that we may view the earlier stratum below John 1:35-49 as a tradition antedating the literary efforts of the evangelist and as a non-Synoptic form of the pericope about the coming of Jesus' first disciples. Moreover, because of the dual accent on "finding" and "coming," it is quite easy to imagine that the earlier form of John 1:35-49 was in fact a sermon which lay, along with others, at the origin of the Johannine community. One can readily envisage that the preacher who painted the dynamic picture of men who come to Jesus and find him to be the Messiah did so in the hope that his hearers would behave in like manner, that they also would *come* to Jesus, and that, *finding* him to be the Messiah, they also would become Christians.

If some of the hearers did so, if the underlying sermon did in part play a role in the origin of the Johannine community, then from where did the converts come? Not from the general world of Greco-Roman culture. There is, of course, a conceptual movement which corresponds to the spatial movement of the verb "to come," and that conceptual movement does not include a step from messianic ignorance to the awakening of messianic expectations. It is not they who have never been told of him who come to see, and it is not they who have never heard of him who come to understand (cf. Is. 52:15; Rom. 15:21). On the contrary, the preacher takes for granted that his hearers already hold certain well-formed messianic expectations, and these expectations constitute in his view a sort of launching pad for a *heilsgeschichtlich* christological trajectory which has its fulfillment in Jesus of Nazareth. *He* is the Mosaic prophet, the eschatological Elijah, the expected Messiah. The preacher of the sermon, therefore, like John the Baptist, points to Jesus, so that those who have been brought up on the traditional Jewish expectations may now *find* the one so long expected.

From these observations it would seem obvious that the preacher was addressing Jews and thus that the homily underlying John 1:35-49 is one of the rare examples within the largely Gentile-Christian New Testament of what Paul referred to as the Gospel of the circumcision (Gal. 2:7). This tells us, in turn, that the evangelization which brought the Johannine community into existence was very probably carried out wholly within the bosom of the synagogue. As regards the Johannine community, "In the beginning was the sermon of the Gospel of the circumcision."

Of course this Gospel of the circumcision will have included considerably more than the account of messianic discovery portrayed in the sermon underlying 1:35-49. There will also have been numerous pieces of Jesus-tradition which were used to support and to make concrete for the hearers the confessions paradigmatically made by Andrew, Peter, Philip, and Nathanael. We cannot know the precise contours of this additional material, but there is good reason to assume that it *included* elements of the passion-resurrection narrative and the early strata of a number of the Johannine miracle stories, several of which may have been collected and shaped under the influence of similar collections which lie behind the Synoptic Gospels, and also under the influence of the Elijah/Elisha cycles in 1 and 2 Kings.[151] In any case, already in this early evangelistic preaching Jesus' miracles were probably called "signs," and it was expected that most Jews who heard and therefore saw these signs would come rather uncritically to believe that Jesus was the promised Messiah.

We may surmise that before a great many years had passed, it occurred to one of the preachers of this inner-synagogue messianic group to collect some of the traditions and homilies into what Ernst Haenchen thought of as a rudimentary, written Gospel.[152] What motivated him to do this? Had he got at least a glimpse of the Gospel of Mark (cf. Lindars' suggestion regarding

---

[151]See R. E. Brown, "Jesus and Elisha", in *Perspective* 12 (1971) 85-104, especially p. 97.

[152]Haenchen's actual words are "What Bultmann called the "Signs Source" can very well have been the gospel of this community: a sort of rudimentary Gospel of Mark. . . ."; p. 303 of *Aus der Literatur zum Johannesevangelium 1929-1956*, in *TR* 23 (1955) 295-335. It may also be pertinent to recall that Haenchen identified as Jewish-Christian the miracle story underlying the first part of John 5; p. 48 of *Johanneische Probleme*, in *ZTK* 56 (1959) 19-54.

what he terms the first edition of John's Gospel)?[153] Or are we to consider the possibility that the Gospel form emerged independently at two junctures in early Christian history? Here we are, I think, in the shadows. In any case, already within the early period, one of the Christian Jews of the inner-synagogue group seems to have penned a document similar, I believe, to the signs source or signs Gospel, which in our time has been spoken of and investigated, to some degree independently of one another, by Rudolph Bultmann, Ernst Haenchen, Robert Fortna, Jürgen Becker, Nikolaus Walter, Willem Nicol, Günther Reim, and Moody Smith.[154] This signs source or signs Gospel was precisely "an essay in christology," which, far from terminating the further formation of oral homilies, clearly now served the author and his preaching colleagues in the task of proclamation.

For our present concerns the importance of the signs source/Gospel lies, of course, in the fact that it affords the historian a glimpse of the messianic group as it lived in the community of the synagogue during the early period. Several notes of importance demand attention:

1. During this period the group's evangelistic preaching seems to have met with considerable success. We may allow for some exaggeration, to be sure. Yet there seem to be genuine reflections of remarkable evangelization in 2:11, 4:53 (note particularly the expression "and he himself believed, and his whole house"), 6:14, etc.; and, by the same token, such dark and pes-

---

[153]B. Lindars, *Behind the Fourth Gospel*, pp. 12f.: "It is likely that John had at least *seen* Mark."

[154]R. Bultmann, *Das Evangelium des Johannes*, and D. Moody Smith, *The Composition and Order of the Fourth Gospel: Bultmann's Literary Theory* (New Haven, 1965); E. Haenchen, the article cited above in note 152, and his unpublished commentary; R. T. Fortna, *The Gospel of Signs*, and a series of redaction-critical essays, the latest being "Christology in the Fourth Gospel: Redaction-Critical Perspectives", in *NTS* 21 (1974-75) 489-504; Jürgen Becker, "Wunder und Christologie", in *NTS* 16 (1969-70) 130-148; N. Walter, "Die Auslegung überlieferter Wundererzählungen im Johannes-Evangelium", in *Theologische Versuche* II (1970) 93-107; W. Nicol, *The Sēmeia in the Fourth Gospel;* G. Reim, *Studien zum alttestamentlichen Hintergrund des Johannesevangeliums;* D. Moody Smith, "The Milieu of the Johannine Miracle Source", in *Jews, Greeks, and Christians* (see note 139 above).

simistic logia as the one in 12:37 are to be assigned literarily to a later stage of the group's history. In the early period the group saw that the Messiah who had come to his own was in fact being widely received among them.

2. It was remembered, to be sure, that in Jerusalem not all of the Messiah's own had received him. Indeed the Johannine evangelists must surely have told the story of Jesus' crucifixion in a way which included inculpating roles played by the authorities of the Jewish people. In recognizing this fact, we are reminded that the preaching of the Christian Gospel was always and everywhere scandalous and offensive. We may also assume, however, that the scandal was focused and accurately defined by midrashic demonstration that in the Messiah's betrayal and death Scripture had been fulfilled.[155]

3. While we can scarcely be certain, it seems that this very early group had for the most part a relatively simple understanding of faith. The signs and the paradoxically scandalous and redemptive proclamation of the passion-resurrection led rather simply to faith, and there was only one level of faith.[156]

4. I have already said that the group was made up altogether of Jews, probably bilingual, but clearly living within the theological, social, and cultural security of the synagogue. In this early period—a period which probably began before the Jewish war, as Moody Smith has recently argued[157]—the group experienced no social dislocation and felt relatively little alienation from their heritage.[158] Here three points in particular demand attention:

---

[155] Cf. John 19:24 etc. and Fortna, *The Gospel of Signs*, pp. 229f.

[156] That the author of the signs source had an understanding of the relationship between signs and faith which was rather different from that of the evangelist is suggested by most of the scholars listed above in note 154. See also an unpublished essay by Paul W. Meyer of Princeton Theological Seminary entitled *Seeing, Signs, and Sources in the Fourth Gospel*.

[157] D. Moody Smith, "Johannine Christianity: Some Reflections on Its Character and Delineation", in *NTS* 21 (1974-75) 222-248, especially p. 246.

[158] Those readers who were in attendance at the (1975) *Journées Bibliques* will recall that this statement elicited some rather spirited disagreement. In what now follows I am responding to the questions raised.

(a) If the group was "at home" within the synagogue, what was its stance toward Torah? The question is difficult to answer with both precision and certainty, but there are several factors which converge to suggest quite strongly that the group was Torah-observant. The traditions of this early period give not the slightest indication that this inner-synagogue group engaged in debates about the validity of Torah; form-critical analysis clearly shows that the references to breach of Sabbath in 5:9. 10. 16. 18 and in 9:14. 16 belong to the later strata, and the same is to be said of the discussion of circumcision and of breach of Sabbath in 7:22ff. Moreover, as we shall shortly see, the group's later exit from the synagogue provides pertinent evidence which points to the conclusion that its members were Torah-observant Jews. It is clear that they desired to remain within the synagogue; their exit was in fact a traumatic expulsion carried out against their will (contrast, e.g., Acts 18:6f.). One does not have the impression of a group which even dreamed of being free from Torah observance. And on what grounds did the authorities expel them? Not on the grounds that the group was lax with regard to Torah observance per se, but rather only on the grounds of their messianic confession of Jesus (9:22, etc.). One is reminded that the *Birkath ha-Minim* seems to have been directed against the confession of Jesus as Messiah, not against discrete breach of Torah.[159] One thinks furthermore of the witness given by the Jewish-Christian author of the "Ascents of James" who says that his community differs from the unbelieving Jews in one regard only: the confession of Jesus as the Christ.[160] And finally one is put in mind of numerous references to law-observant Jewish Christians in the Acts of the Apostles. Note in particular the words which Luke allows the elders of the Jerusalem church to speak to Paul:

> You see, brother, how many thousands there are among the Jews of those who have believed; they are all zealous for the law. . . . (Acts 21:20).

---

[159] Martyn, *History and Theology*, Chapter 2.

[160] Clementine Recognitions 1, 43. 2; B. Rehm, *Die Pseudoklementinen II, Rekognitionen in Rufins Übersetzung* (GCS, 51) (Berlin, 1965). For the source analysis of the *Ascent of James* see G. Strecker, *Das Judenchristentum in den Pseudoklementinen,* pp. 221ff, and above chapter two.

Whatever the precise stance toward Torah may have been in the case of Jesus,[161] we have every reason to believe that numerous Jewish-Christian groups were quite observant of Torah. And the pertinent data in the Fourth Gospel indicate that in its early period the Johannine group was probably a case in point.

(b) If the group was "at home" in the synagogue, what stance did it take toward the Gentile mission? Regarding this question the early strata in the Gospel are utterly silent. I see, in fact, no indication that in the early period the Johannine group even had any knowledge of the mission to the Gentiles. To be sure, one must bear in mind that this period stretched from a relatively early date to some point in the eighties. That fact alone may be judged as sufficient grounds for concluding that the group knew of the Gentile mission. Could Christians in any locale and of any sort have lived into the eighties ignorant of that momentous and vigorously debated development? Nevertheless, it is the marks of the vigorous debate which are most notably absent. As is always the case, one must exercise great caution in the interpretation of silence. I shall only suggest that whatever the Johannine group knew of the mission among the Gentiles, it would seem that they somehow managed to avoid being drawn into debates about it. And that suggestion brings us back to the major point: In the early period the group experienced no social dislocation and felt little alienation from their Jewish heritage.

(c) One is not surprised, therefore, to observe that in the strata pertinent to the early period there are no notes of dualism[162] and no indications of world-foreignness. I have already pointed out that Jesus' crucifixion, with its midrashic explication, served to focus the offensive character of the good news. It must have been recognized that the Gospel—even this Gospel

---

[161] It is of course a non sequitur to argue that the Johannine group's attitude toward Torah must have been such and such because Jesus' attitude was such and such. We must proceed on the basis of data in the Fourth Gospel.

[162] Cf. J. Becker, "Beobachtungen zum Dualismus im Johannesevangelium", in *ZNW* 65 (1974) 71-87, an attempt to show that the Johannine dualism had a history of development within the Johannine community: "The thinking characteristic of the earliest phase is pre-dualistic" (85).

of the circumcision—was not an announcement of the continuation of "life as usual." On the contrary, God's long-awaited, eschatological prophet-Messiah had come to grant genuinely new deliverance to his people. We must also note, however, that the Johannine evangelists seem clearly to have proclaimed the "new" without introducing such radical categories of discontinuity as are associated with dualism and world-foreignness. In the early strata Jesus himself, far from being a stranger, is quite plainly the expected Jewish Messiah. Correspondingly, the early homily and the signs Gospel itself indicate no feelings of suspicion, fear, or hostility toward the messianic group on the part of the Jewish authorities. In short, however theologically revolutionary their message must have been, the group was able to view the synagogue as the primary expression of the properly ordered kosmos.

5. I have referred above to the signs Gospel as an essay in christology. In fact, its massive concentration on the christology of the miracle worker produced a picture of the Messiah so numinous that that picture was destined in time to assume the proportions of "God striding across the face of the earth."[163] In the early period, however, there seems to have been no fear that such a christology could pose a threat to monotheism. On the contrary, we see in this period only *a group of Christian Jews*[164] who stand in a relatively untroubled stream of social and theological continuity precisely within the synagogue.

## II. THE MIDDLE PERIOD

*Part of the Group Is Born as a Separate Community by
Experiencing Two Major Traumas:
Excommunication from the Synagogue and Martyrdom*

---

[163] The expression is derived, of course, from ones coined by F. C. Baur; E. Käsemann has suggestively revived the expression in our time. See, e.g., *The Testament of Jesus*, pp. 8f (German ed., p. 22).

[164] Here and later the reader will see that I have tried to grasp certain aspects of the history of the Johannine community by two means: a

In the course of the middle period there were momentous developments and alterations, both in the group's setting and within the group itself. The history of the Johannine tradition is particularly revealing here, for in contrast to the relatively tranquil waters which lie behind the earliest homily and the signs Gospel, one sees reflected in the next stages of tradition rather complex and stormy seas. The middle period is marked off, indeed, by the fact that the authorities now began to be quite suspicious of the rapidly growing messianic group, and both they and some rank-and-file synagogue members demanded that the group prove the validity of its messianic proclamation on the basis of exegesis. There ensued a number of midrashic debates, and in the course of the debates there emerged a widening spectrum of opinion about the group's message, ranging from absolute commitment (6:68) to partial faith (2:23ff., etc.) to outright unbelief (7:12. 47, etc.).[165]

And beyond such sobering developments lay two major traumas suffered by the messianic group and rather clearly reflected in dramatic expansions of two of the earlier miracle stories.

## The First Trauma

In the dramatic expansion of the story of the man born blind (Jn. 9)—a dramatic expansion which may originally have been composed orally—we can see a clear reflection of the first trauma. Not far into the middle period the rapid growth of the messianic group caused the authorities not only to be suspicious, but also to take a radical step designed to terminate the flow of converts into the group. They introduced the reworded *Birkath ha-Minim* into the synagogue service in order to be able to iden-

---

distinction between "group" and "community," and a distinction between "Christian Jews" and "Jewish Christians." The possibility that the Beloved Disciple was an historical person who played a role in the early period cannot be pursued in the present book.

[165] It is not my intention to suggest that differences of opinion arose overnight in the middle period or that there was absolute unanimity in the early period.

tify and excommunicate those who confessed Jesus as Messiah (9:22. 34).[166]

From the logion of 12:42 and indeed from the role played by the blind man's parents in Chapter 9, it is clear that to a degree this step had the desired effect. Some of the members of the messianic group, and perhaps even more of those who were merely inclined toward the messianic faith, turned away from the confession in order to remain safely within the community of the synagogue. We shall return to these persons at a later point. Many members of the messianic group, however, paid the price of their convictions and suffered excommunication. From this point forward we may refer to these people, I think, as *the Johannine community*, for it is obvious that the outworking of the *Birkath ha-Minim* in the city in question changed the Johannine circle— against their will—from a messianic *group* within the synagogue into a separate *community* outside that social and theological setting. In this trauma the members suffered not only social dislocation but also great alienation, for the synagogue/world which had been their social and theological womb, affording nurture and security, was not only removed, but even became the enemy who persecutes. We may surmise that the roots of the dualistic patterns of thought and of the world-foreignness which came to full fruition only later are to be traced, in fact, to the sufferings of this middle period.

## The Second Trauma

As I have said above, the use of the reworded *Birkath ha-Minim* narrowed the flow of converts, but it clearly did not terminate the flow altogether. The authorities therefore concluded that further restrictive measures were necessary, and in light of the Johannine community's increasing tendency to view Jesus as a numinous and somewhat other-worldly figure, the authorities were apparently able to argue that confession of such a figure constituted not only unacceptable messianism, but also a violation of monotheism (5:18). In short, they were able not only to

---

[166]Martyn, *History and Theology*, Chapter 2.

excommunicate those who confessed Jesus as Messiah, but also to arrest some of the evangelists from the separated community and to subject them to trial and, indeed to execution as *Messithim/Planoi* (seducers), as ditheists who led other Jews into the worship of a second god alongside Adonai.[167]

It is not difficult to see that this second trauma deepened the community's fear and distrust. Johannine evangelists were now not only socially dislocated and alienated. They were also subjected to the possibility of being "snatched away" out of life (cf. 10:28f.; 15:18). It is here that we may see what Wayne Meeks has suggestively termed a harmonic reinforcement between social experience and christology.[168] Expelled from the synagogue, the Johannine community was bound to search for a mature interpretation of the expulsion, and that search led it to new christological formulations. The logos hymn, for example, is probably to be assigned to this middle period, and its wording may very well reflect the rude awakening of the twin traumas:

The Messiah came to his own world,
and his own people did *not* receive him.[169]

---

[167]*Ibid.*, chp. 3. Note furthermore the use of the verb t' ' in the Syriac text of Clementine Recognitions i, 62.1; W. Frankenberg, *Die syrischen Clementinen mit griechischen Paralleltext*. The passage is discussed in some detail in Chapter 2 of the present volume.

[168]Wayne A. Meeks, *The Man From Heaven in Johannine Sectarianism*, in *JBL* 91 (1972) 44-72, especially p. 71. A similar point is made by David E. Aune, *The Cultic Setting of Realized Eschatology in Early Christianity* (note 137 above). Aune unfortunately takes the additional step, however, of repeatedly using expressions which suggest that the flow was unidirectional: *from* social experience *to* christology. For example, "The Johannine Jesus was relevant for the faith and life of the community primarily because he was the personification and embodiment of the religious needs, values and aspirations of the community projected onto and superimposed over the historical Jesus" (p. 101). Later on the same page: ". . . the Johannine Jesus is in reality a reflection of the salvific needs and ideals of the community. . . ." One can easily imagine the fourth evangelist shuddering at such statements. Recall John 1:18, 3:13, 3:31-36, 6:44, etc.

[169]The interpretation of John 1:11 is one of those points at which a hermeneutical rule attributed orally by E. Käsemann to W. Bauer is of

The *heilsgeschichtlich* pattern of thought presupposed in the earlier christological trajectory from traditional expectations to their fulfillment in Jesus is now being significantly altered by the dualistic, above/below pattern.

To be sure, the Messiah is none other than the eternal sophia-logos through whom God created all that is; yet after the two major traumas, the community began to perceive that he came to his own world/synagogue as the stranger from above.[170] This perception *may* be reflected, moreover, in certain aspects of the Gospel's theological geography. If Judea is the Messiah's "native land," the locus of those who were originally "his own," and the place where his teaching had to be given, then there may be considerable significance in the indications that it was impossible for Jesus to "remain" there. That is to say, the Johannine community, having found it impossible to remain in the synagogue, may have perceived a prefiguring of that development in the geography of the Messiah's story.[171] In any case, in the middle period the community began to take *onto itself* with increasing intensity the characteristics of the stranger from above.[172] Socially, having been excommunicated and having subsequently experienced persecution to the death, they no longer find their

---

crucial importance: Before one inquires into the author's intention, he must ask how the first readers are likely to have understood the text. In light of the history of the Johannine community (not to mention the history of other communities as reflected in Mark 12:1-12 and Romans 9:1ff.), one may be virtually certain that the first readers and hearers understood John 1:11 as a reference to contemporary Jewish unbelief. The author of that verse took no steps to exclude this obvious interpretation. It follows that he probably intended it. (We may also note that he did not balance his reference to Jewish unbelief with a reference to the Gentile mission, as was done by the traditioners behind Mark 12:1-12, Luke 14:15-24, etc.)

[170] Again I have borrowed a note from the uncommonly perceptive article by Wayne A. Meeks, "The Man from Heaven". Cf. also E. Käsemann, *The Testament of Jesus*, p. 22: ". . . the stranger from the world above. . . ."

[171] The interpretation of John 4:44 is notoriously difficult. See R. E. Brown, *John, ad loc,* and contrast R. T. Fortna, "Theological Use of Locale in the Fourth Gospel," in *Anglican Theological Review* Suppl. Series 3 (1974) 95-112.

[172] Again cf. both Meeks and Aune as cited above in note 168.

origin and their intelligible point of departure in the synagogue and in its traditions. On the contrary, they, like their Christ, become people who are not "of the world" and who are for that reason hated by the world. In this process they cease, in fact, to be *Christian Jews* and become instead *Jewish Christians*. To express it theologically, they cease even to be "Jews" and become instead—like Nathanael—"truly Israelites" who now constitute the *new* "his own" because the stranger has come from above and has chosen them out of the world/synagogue.

## III. The Late Period

*Movement Toward Firm Social and Theological Configurations*

The history of the traditions and of the literary activity proper to the late period brings us not only to further homilies, but also to the climactic writing of the fully Johannine Gospel in its first and second editions.[173] The period also finds the Johannine community forming its own theology and its own identity not only vis-à-vis the parent synagogue, but also in relation to other Christian groups in its setting.[174] The period is, thus, extraordinarily rich and complex, and could easily form in its own right the subject for several essays. Because of the present need for brevity, I shall concentrate attention in the remaining space on three expressions, the first of which reaches back into the middle period, and the other two of which appear to be significantly revealing of developments during this late period. The three expressions are:

1. the disciples of Moses (9:28);
2. the Jews who had believed in him (8:31);
3. the other sheep (10:16).

---

[173] Cf. the five-stage analysis made by R. E. Brown as cited above in note 136. Contrary to Lindars' own opinion I find his analysis of two major editions to be quite harmonious with the hypothesis of a signs source/Gospel: B. Lindars, *The Gospel of John*, pp. 46ff.

[174] Cf. R. E. Brown, "Other Sheep Not of This Fold: The Johannine Perspective on Christian Diversity in the Late First Century," *JBL* 97 (1978) 5-22.

## 1. The Disciples of Moses

One scarcely needs to emphasize the importance of the term "disciples" for our attempts to discern the community behind the Gospel. In fact, not only significant aspects of the community's life in general, but also glimpses of the *history* of the community are revealed in the ways in which this term is employed in the various strata.

In the earliest evangelistic sermons and in the signs Gospel, where the term seems to have been employed a number of times, the word "disciples" was apparently used in only two formulations: "disciples of John" and "disciples of Jesus." Moreover, the role of the disciples of John was quite clear. They were on stage, so to speak, in order to become disciples of Jesus in order to exemplify the movement which persons experience by *becoming* disciples of Jesus. That movement was characterized, as we have already seen, by simple and largely unquestioned continuity. Jesus was the prophet-Messiah foretold by Moses (1:45). Hence, while one who became a disciple of Jesus would cease actively to be a disciple of the Baptist, he would nevertheless move along a line which stands in unquestioned continuity with the witness and writings of Moses. Far from abandoning Moses, he would simply have attached himself to the one of whom Moses wrote.

In the middle period, as we have noted, that simple and unquestioned *heilsgeschichtlich* continuity was decisively shattered. In the face of numerous conversions within the synagogue, the Jewish authorities felt that they had to take drastic steps. Quite naturally, these repressive steps had ultimately to be based on Moses, and that fact led the authorities to combine their use of the *Birkath ha-Minim* with a midrashic attack. This combination, in turn, led to a startlingly new "either . . . or." In the excommunication drama of John 9, when the Jews are asked by the formerly blind man whether they wish to become disciples of Jesus, they answer angrily,

You are his disciple; but we are disciples of Moses (9:28).

In the middle period in which this drama was formulated, the authorities obviously laid down a new dictum. *Either* one is a loyal disciple of Moses, remaining true to the ancient Jewish community, *or* one has become a disciple of Jesus, thereby ceasing to be a disciple of Moses.

To the original, inner-synagogue group of Christian Jews, who knew Jesus to be the one of whom Moses wrote, this formulation must have come as a great shock. It is clear, however, that before long the shock would have not only to be endured, but also to be interpreted. What is the true meaning of this newly formulated "either . . . or"?

It is quite clear that the members of the original group of Christian Jews did not all perceive the new "either . . . or" in the same way, and correspondingly their experiences of it and the stances they developed toward it were rather varied. It hardly needs to be said once again that the Johannine community experienced it in the form of excommunication. It is equally clear, as I have also said earlier, that the same was not true of all members of the original messianic group. Some managed to remain within the bosom of the synagogue by presenting themselves in public as disciples of Moses and children of Abraham, while considering themselves in private to be *also* disciples of Jesus. A Johannine logion probably to be assigned to the middle period refers to these people as persons who have believed in Jesus, but who, in order to avoid excommunication, refused to make a public confession of that belief (12:42). And in another logion (6:66) one hears similarly that many of the original messianic group "turned back" and did not keep the kind of social company which would make their confession public. Perhaps we may refer to these people as believing Jews who wish to remain Christian Jews, but who are determined to do so in secret. Such a suggestion leads us to take up the next expression.

## 2. The Jews Who Had Believed in Him

With this expression we return to the late period, for it occurs in a homily (8:31ff.) which was probably composed in that period. The modern critical judgment to delete the words "the Jews who had believed in him" as a gloss[175] has no manuscript support, and may be in fact one of the numerous judgments which reflect our generally inadequate knowledge of the varieties of Christian Jews and Jewish Christians in the period after 70 A.D.

Bearing in mind a pregnant suggestion made in 1932 by Schwartz to the effect that the Johannine polemic often becomes understandable as a reaction against some form of Jewish Christianity, we may proceed not by deleting the troublesome phrase, but by inquiring for the precise identity of these Jews who have for some time believed in Jesus.[176]

It is a distinct service of C. H. Dodd to have made a strong case for the thesis that the evangelist refers here to Jewish Christians of his own time,[177] but Dodd's thesis needs also to be strengthened and in various regards corrected.[178]

From the description of Jesus' interlocutors, and from the mouths of the interlocutors themselves, there are numerous indications that they represent, in fact, not Jewish Christians, but rather Christian Jews who wish proudly to hold some sort of dual allegiance. Let me mention five observations:

1. One must reiterate the straightforward identification in verse 31 which finds, as Dodd showed, significant parallels in instances in Acts where the perfect participle of "to believe"

---

[175] After incorrectly crediting Dodd and Brown with this view, Lindars states it as his own: *The Gospel of John, ad loc.*, and *Behind the Fourth Gospel*, p. 80. Dodd's argument was constructed by accepting the text as it stands (see note 177 below); Brown suggested that verse 31 and the troublesome phrase in verse 32 be allotted to the final redactor: *John, ad loc.*

[176] E. Schwartz, "Unzeitgemässe Beobachtungen zu den Clementinen", in *ZNW* 31 (1932) 191.

[177] C. H. Dodd, "A l'arrière-plan d'un dialogue johannique", in *Revue d'histoire et de philosophie religieuses*, 37 (1957) 5-17; *Behind a Johannine Dialogue*, in *More New Testament Studies* (Manchester, 1968), pp. 41-57.

[178] See particularly Rudolf Schnackenburg, *Das Johannesevangelium*, II. Teil, Freiburg, 1971, pp. 258ff; Bruce Schein, *Our Father Abraham*, Yale Dissertation, Ann Arbor, Michigan (microfilm), 1972; Gilbert Bartholomew, *An Early Christian Sermon-Drama: John 8:31-59*, Columbia University-Union Theological Seminary Dissertation, Ann Arbor, Michigan (microfilm), 1974.

emerges. One of these has already commanded our attention: "those among the Jews who had believed" (21:20). Note, moreover, the syntax of the expression in John 8:31; *here* the participle "those who had believed" is adjectival, merely modifying the noun "the Jews."

2. These people characterize themselves as "descendants of Abraham" (vv. 33 and 39). While this designation could be claimed by any Jew, the group's identification in verse 31 as "the Jews who had believed in him" should remind us of the evidence in Paul's letters suggesting that the expression "descendants of Abraham" was used as a self-designation among early Christian Jews (2 Cor. 11:22; cf. Gal. 3:6-29).[179]

3. It follows easily that in John 8 this self-designation may have had at least two points of reference. The interlocutors could have linked their existence as Christians with being "descendants of Abraham," but *antecedently* they are descendants of Abraham precisely because they are Jews. Perhaps they would be happy to call themselves "descendants of Abraham" particularly because it could be a phrase with ambiguity. To the ears of the Jewish authorities it would mean only that those who use it are loyal Jews, while to the users themselves it could also be a secret expression of their Christian inclinations. In any case, when the issue of freedom arises, they proudly call on their blood descendance from Abraham to show that they have never been enslaved. Impressed as they are with Jesus' word (v. 30), they do not need *it* to make them free.

4. One notes also their proud and indeed polemical claim to the inheritance of monotheism. *Others* may move in the direction of a christology which approaches ditheism, a form of apostasy from Adonai, symbolized as being born of fornication or adultery.[180] *They* emphatically remain monotheists, as the syntax of verse 41b makes clear: "We have *one* father: God."

5. But we may note that, at least initially, it appears to be only the high christology, and only the absolute claims for Christ,

---

[179] See the pertinent discussion in the work of B. Schein as cited in the preceding note.

[180] Note the comments to John 8:41 made by R. E. Brown, *John, ad loc.*

which are offensive to these Christian Jews. For them Jesus may be allowed to stand *within Heilsgeschichte*, within the prophetic line, and while that means that he is not greater than Abraham and the prophets (v. 53), it nevertheless means that he is to be affirmed *along with them*. At some point these Christian Jews have desired to take their stand both on their Jewish descent and on Jesus' word.

This intention to hold a dual allegiance seems, moreover, to be clearly reflected in the polemic formulated by the Johannine preacher responsible for this homily. Formal analysis of his sermon shows that both of the first two major sections begin with a highly emphatic reference to Jesus' word (vv. 31 and 37).

*Verse 31*

The expression "in my word" not only employs the emphatic pronoun, but also stands syntactically in the emphatic position. Given the context, one might paraphrase the protasis:

If you take a constant stand absolutely in *my* word. . . .

And the apodosis significantly employs the adverb "truly" which is nowhere else linked with the construction "to be disciples." Thus, a further paraphrase:

You Jews who have believed in me! If you take a constant stand absolutely in *my* word, you are *truly* my disciples. . . .

What would seem to be the alternative? Either to take one's stand in the word of someone else—an interpretation which would conflict with verse 30—or to attempt, as I have just suggested, to stand simultaneously and more or less equally in the words of Jesus and in the words of another teacher. In that case, implies the preacher, one is not *truly* a disciple of Jesus.

It is here, indeed, that we catch a clear glimpse of the community's considered interpretation—in the late period—of the "either . . . or" formulated some time earlier by the Jewish authorities. Shocked as the Johannine community must initially

have been to hear it said that one must be either a disciple of
Moses or a disciple of Jesus, they necessarily had eventually to
interpret that formulation not only in the light of their own heritage from ancient Israel, but also in the light of the behavior of
their former colleagues who, in view of the threat of excommunication, tried secretly to maintain a dual allegiance. Given this
latter development, the Johannine community perceived that *Jesus' word* had to be granted absolute priority, and that only on the
basis of his word could one understand the witness borne to him
by the Fathers. Thus it was that the Johannine preacher heard
Jesus declare with divine solemnity:

Before Abraham was I am (8:58).

In place of the *heilsgeschichtlich* christology "from behind,"[181] we now find the full emergence of the dualistic christology "from above." Indeed, the initially shocking "either . . . or,"
formulated so polemically by the Jewish authorities, is now
turned back on them and on the so-called Christian Jews by being
interpreted quite radically in dualistic terms.

From the point of view of the Johannine community it is
quite insufficient to say that one is either a disciple of Moses or a
disciple of Jesus. Rather one is *either* from above—from
God—*or* one is from below—from the devil.

*Verse 37*

Here the believing Jews, the "descendants of Abraham," are
said to have taken the wrong path as a result of the fact that "my
word finds no room among you." It is in this second section that
"the Jews who had believed in him" prove to be fundamentally
undistinguishable from "the Jews" in general, in preparation for
verse 48 where they are, in fact, so identified. But *ex hypothesi*

---

[181] For this suggestive expression I am indebted to Dr. Adriaan
Krijger, a pastor-theologian in The Hague and one of my stimulating
colleagues during an unforgettable period at the Ecumenical Institute for
Advanced Theological Studies in Jerusalem, 1974-75.

this means only that, from the point of view of the separated Johannine community, the attempt on the part of these secret believers, these so-called Christian Jews, to straddle the fence is wholly unsuccessful; their attempt constitutes, in fact, what Wayne Meeks has correctly characterized as a diabolic lie.[182] Because they do not take their stand absolutely in the word of Jesus, they only prove that his word does not have any place at all among them, and that in the final analysis they are not "the Jews who had believed in him," but merely "the Jews."

*Theologically* it is therefore no cause for surprise to the Johannine community when these former colleagues of theirs turn out to be horribly instrumental in the martyrdom of some of the Johannine evangelists, presumably by functioning as informers intent on preserving monotheism (vv. 37, 40, 44, 59).

In the present context I cannot offer further analysis. I can only summarize by suggesting that together with 2:23ff., 11:46 and 12:42, the homily of 8:31ff. forms one of several references to a group whose distinct identity emerged in the late period, and whom, following the syntax of 8:31, we ought carefully to characterize not as Jewish Christians, but rather as Christian Jews. Indeed, in light of the foregoing analysis, one might suggest a final paraphrase of 8:31 as follows:

Jesus then said to those who understood themselves to be Christian Jews: If you take a constant stand absolutely in my word, you will be genuinely liberated as Jewish Christians.

The point is that with the emergence in the late period of this group of Christian Jews, the social configuration in which the Johannine community finds itself is not completely grasped when one speaks of the polarity vis-à-vis the parent synagogue. The social configuration is more complex; it is at least trilateral, involving first the parent synagogue, second the group of secretly Christian Jews who have been able to remain within the synagogue, and third the separated Johannine community, a

---

[182]Wayne A. Meeks, "The Man From Heaven" (note 168), p. 69.

community made up almost wholly of Jewish Christians (also a few Samaritan Christians[183]).

Our last question is whether even this trilateral configuration is adequate as a representation of the social complexity of the late period. And the posing of this question leads us finally to the expression in 10:16.

## 3. The Other Sheep

Aside from Chapter 10 the word "sheep" occurs in the Fourth Gospel only four times—twice in the pericope of the temple cleansing and twice in Chapter 21. In Chapter 10 it occurs no less than fifteen times, and it is obviously used in ways which are quite revealing as regards the history of the Johannine community.

Notice first that the word is distributed throughout most of Chapter 10. In the parables at the opening of the chapter (vv. 1-5) the word "sheep" appears five times, and in the explanations which follow these parables the word appears another seven times. Finally, leaving aside verse 16 for the moment, the word emerges twice more in verses 26 and 27. In all fourteen instances the primary reference is quite clear. The sheep stand in the first instance for the Johannine community.

a. It is they who hear the voice of the Good Shepherd and who follow him; and it is they whom he calls by name.

b. It is they who flee from alternative shepherds and who refuse to listen to them because they do not recognize the voices of those shepherds.

c. It is they whose lives are threatened by the wolf when he comes to snatch them away and to scatter them; and it is they who, when they are thus endangered, are abandoned by the hired hand, who chooses to avoid the possibility of his own death by leaving the community behind.

d. And, finally, it is they who receive the absolute assurance

---

[183] On the whole I find convincing the interpretation of John 4:10-15 offered by H. Leroy, *Rätsel und Missverständnis*, pp. 88-99. See the review by R. E. Brown, in *Biblica* 51 (1970) 152-154.

from the Good Shepherd that, however threatened they may be, no one will ever be able actually to snatch them out of his hand or out of the hand of his Father.

I should not want to claim that it is the only viable interpretation, but in light of the history of the Johannine community which has emerged in the foregoing analyses, I am led at least to suggest that the parables and their interpretations must be taken together as an allegory, in the reading of which those who were initiates by virtue of having shared a common history—that is to say, the members of the Johannine community—would easily recognize the following representations:

1. the sheep    stand for the Johannine community.

2. strangers    stand for the Jewish authorities ("the
   thieves       Pharisees" of Chapter 9) who in fact kill, de-
   robbers      stroy, snatch away, and scatter the Johan-
   the wolf     nine community.

3. hireling     may stand for the secretly believing "rulers"
   who avoid the possibility of their own execution by abandoning the Johannine community when it is endangered.

4. the Good   stands for Jesus, as he is active through
   Shepherd  Johannine evangelists who are prepared to
   face martyrdom for the community and who
   both receive and transmit this absolute assurance that, however threatening the Jewish
   authorities may become, they shall never be
   able to snatch any member of the community
   out of the hands of Jesus and of the Father.

We come now to verse 16. If we accept the wording of papyrus 66, the text reads:

And I have other sheep, that are not of this fold.
I must gather them also,

and they will heed my voice,
and there will be one flock, one shepherd.


The problems are numerous. In the present setting we can consider only one: Who are the "other sheep"?

The dominant answer, given by Bultmann, Barrett, Schnackenburg, Brown, and Lindars, is to identify the "other sheep" as Gentiles who will believe as a result of the Gentile mission.[184] In light of the common opinion of these five exegetes the least one can say is that this interpretation may be correct.

There are, however, certain factors which indicate a different interpretation, as Hans Joachim Schoeps suggested a number of years ago, and as H. B. Kossen has more recently suggested, apparently without being influenced by the views of Schoeps.[185] Could it be that the other sheep are Jewish Christians belonging to conventicles known to but separate from the Johannine community? Let us return to the text, taking it one clause at a time. Several points seem either quite clear or at least probable:


1.   "I have other sheep"
These other sheep already exist. The reader or hearer is simply informed of their existence.

2.   "that are not of this fold"
How will the Johannine community have understood "this fold"? Up to this point in Chapter 10 every reference to sheep has been a reference to them. It is their community, therefore, which is "this fold."

3.   "I must gather (or lead) them also"
We cannot be sure of the text, of course, but I think the motif of unification which is so strong in the last clause of the

---

[184]See the commentaries of these scholars, *ad loc*.

[185]H. J. Schoeps, *Jewish Christianity*, p. 131; H. B. Kossen, "Who Were the Greeks of John XII 20?", in *Studies in John* (J. N. Sevenster Festschrift, Leiden, 1970), pp. 97-110, especially pp. 107f. Cf. also M. L. Appold, *The Oneness Motif in the Fourth Gospel* (Tübingen, 1976), pp. 11, 262ff.

verse provides weighty support for the reading of P66.[186]
One may also note that P66 preserved, almost alone, the
correct reading in John 7:52. I shall return to the interpretation of this clause.

4.    "and they will heed my voice,
      and there will be one flock, one shepherd."

The prophecies with which the verse closes strongly
emphasize unification. The gathering of the "other sheep"
will lead to there being one flock under one shepherd.

We may take our bearings, I think, from this emphatic
prophecy of unification, which is obviously the goal of the entire
logion. And that leads us, as regards the identity of the other
sheep, to return to the clause, "I must gather them also."

Why, we may ask, should there be such an emphasis on
unification, and why for the sake of the unification must the other
sheep be *gathered*?

The obvious answer is that they have been scattered. Are
there indications that such is, in fact, the case?

The posing of this question takes us first to John 11:52, for
that verse—the ironic prophecy of Caiaphas—is very closely
bound to 10:16 by these same two motifs: unification, and the
gathering which leads to unification. The important point to
notice is that 11:52 also contains the word "scatter abroad" in the
expression "the children of God who are scattered abroad." If one
takes seriously *all* of the elements of 11:52 and their deep roots in
both the traumas and the hopes of exilic and post-exilic Judaism,
he may be led to the following interpretation: The high priest of all
Jews is made to prophesy that Jesus will die in behalf of the
Jewish nation both in its homeland and in its scattering, its dispersion.[187]

Now, returning to John 10, we note, interestingly enough,

---

[186] For the contrary judgment see R. Schnackenburg, *Das Johannesevangelium, ad loc.*; by implication W. A. Meeks accepted the reading of P66: *The Prophet-King*, p. 318n: ". . . the reference in 10:16 about
'other sheep' which must be 'gathered'. . . ."

[187] Interpretative opinion on John 11:52 is sharply divided. W. C.
van Unnik, J. A. T. Robinson, A. F. J. Klijn, and L. van Hartingsveld

the presence of the verb "scatter" in verse 12. In the picture of the wolf the Johannine community is reminded that the Jewish authorities scatter those who are the sheep of the Good Shepherd. To what, precisely, does this refer? In all probability it is a Johannine *reinterpretation* of the widespread and classic motif of Jewish dispersion. *In the experience of the Johannine community* the scattering of the sheep occurred when the *Birkath ha-Minim* was imposed in their city.

It seems probable, however, that under Jamnian authority the *Birkath ha-Minim* was in fact introduced over a wide geographical area.[188] It follows, I think, that the portrait of the "other sheep" is drawn in such a way as to refer *primarily* to other Jewish Christians who, like those of the Johannine community, have been *scattered* from their parent synagogues by experiencing excommunication. It is, then, a vision of the Johannine community that the day will come when all of the conventicles of scattered Jewish Christians will be gathered into one flock under the one Good Shepherd.

If these interpretative suggestions have some merit, we may

---

read the verse very much as I have suggested (bibliographical data given on p. 106 of the article by H. B. Kossen cited above in note 185). C. K Barrett, R. Schnackenburg, and R. E. Brown, on the other hand, represent commentators who argue for a reference to the Gentile mission. It seems to me that Schnackenburg and Brown do not read the verse in its own right, but rather interpret it against its grain because they have already judged 10:16 to contain a reference to the Gentile mission.

[188] The *Birkath ha-Minim* was one of the "ordinances" issued from Jamnia. On the ordinances in general see J. Neusner, *A Life of Rabban Yohanan Ben Zakkai* (Leiden, 1962), pp. 155ff.; Neusner, *Development of a Legend* (Leiden, 1970), pp. 206ff.; J. Goldin, "The Period of the Talmud" in Vol. 1 of L. Finkelstein, ed., *The Jews: Their History, Culture, and Religion* (New York, 1949). To make decisions regarding the synagogue liturgy was one of the major prerogatives claimed by the Jamnia academy in its attempt to supply stability and cohesiveness in the post-war period, and Berakoth 28b (cf. j Berakoth 8a) explicitly identifies the *Birkath ha-Minim* as one of the stabilizing ordinances. It is true that the claims to authority made by the Jamnia academy were resented in some quarters, but the specific ordinances known to us seem generally to have been recognized. See also the discussion in Martyn, *History and Theology*, pp. 32-41, and Justin, *Dialogue*, 16 and 17, cf. Eusebius, *H. E.* iv, 18, 7.

conclude this rather brief and fragmentary historical *sketch* by suggesting that by the time the Fourth Gospel itself was written, the social and theological configuration in which the Johannine community found itself was in fact not trilateral but rather at least quadrilateral:

1. We see first, of course, the Johannine community.

2. We see, second, that the Johannine community is sharply differentiated from the parent synagogue, to the point, in fact, of being polarized with a breakdown in communication—John 3:11 and 15:18ff. The synagogue and its "Jews" form the clearest representation of the alien "world."

3. We see, third, that the community is, if anything, even more sharply differentiated and alienated from a group of so-called Christian Jews who remain within the synagogue—John 8:31ff. and 12:42—and who are therefore "of this world."

4. But we see also, fourth, that the Johannine community is aware of the existence of other communities of Jewish Christians who have also suffered excommunication and with whom there is the hope of unification.[189]

One final word. To most interpreters, John 7:35 and 12:20 are clear references to Greeks who will come to believe via the Gentile mission;[190] similarly the title accorded to Jesus by the Samaritans—Savior of the world—is thought to indicate a vision of universality; and in any case there can be no doubt that the picture of Peter in Chapter 21 as shepherd and (Roman?) martyr—to say nothing of data in the Johannine epistles pertinent to the development of "early Catholicism"—indicates a relationship with the emerging "great Church" which lives on the frontier of the Gentile mission. It remains to be said, however, that if the quadrilateral picture of social and theological relationships which I have just sketched is accurate, and if the earlier glimpses I have offered are generally valid, then the history of the Johannine

---

[189] Concerning the number of groups in the Johannine purview see also R. E. Brown, "Other Sheep" (note 174 above).

[190] See, as examples, R. Schnackenburg, *Das Johannesevangelium*, II. Teil, *ad loc.*; R. E. Brown, *John*, pp. lxxvii f. and *ad loc.*

community from its origin through the period of its life in which the Fourth Gospel was composed forms to no small extent a chapter in the history of *Jewish* Christianity.[191]

---

[191] Unfortunately the learned book by O. Cullmann, *Der johanneische Kreis* (Tübingen, 1975), came into my hands too late to be used in the writing of this chapter. As always, I find numerous aspects of Cullmann's work to be helpfully instructive. Were there time and space here, I should like especially to pursue the questions which arise from a comparison of the Johannine community with the Jewish-Christian communities reflected in discrete strata of the Pseudo-Clementines. Cf. Cullmann, *op. cit.*, pp. 62-66 and Chapter 2 of the present volume.

# APPENDIX

# The Pseudo-Clementine Recognitions
# Book One, Chapters 33-71

The Pseudo-Clementines were originally written in Greek, and for the *Homilies* we have good Greek manuscripts and a critically edited text: B. Rehm, *Die Pseudoklementinen I* (Homilien), *GCS* 42 (Berlin, 1953). In the case of the *Recognitions* we are dependent on (a) a Latin translation made in the early fifth century by Rufinus, who surely thought he was translating a Greek text originally written by Clement of Rome, and (b) a Syriac translation of Books 1-4 also made from a Greek text and stemming from the same general period. To facilitate the reader's grasp of the arguments presented in Chapter 2 of the present volume I provide here the standard English translation of *Recognitions* 1, 33-71. It was made for the *Ante-Nicene Fathers* by Thomas Smith from the Latin text available to him in the 1880's, and for a general comprehension of the text it is quite adequate.

The scholar who wishes to pursue some points in detail will be able to work with the critical edition of the Latin text by B. Rehm, *Die Pseudoklementinen II* (Rekognitionen in Rufins Übersetzung), *GCS* 51 (Berlin, 1956) and to consult the Syriac given in W. Frankenburg, *Die syrischen Clementinen mit griechischen Paralleltext* (Berlin, 1937). Frankenburg's rendering of the Syriac into Greek, while a genuine aid, is unreliable at points. See also the text-critical and interpretative comments presented in G. Strecker, *Judenchristentum*, 221-254.

## CHAP. 33—ABRAHAM: HIS POSTERITY.

"Therefore Abraham, when he was desirous to learn the    1
causes of things, and was intently pondering upon what had been
told him, the true Prophet appeared to him, who alone knows the
hearts and purpose of men, and disclosed to him all things which    2
he desired. He taught him the knowledge of the Divinity; intimated the origin of the world, and likewise its end; showed him
the immortality of the soul, and the manner of life which was
pleasing to God; declared also the resurrection of the dead, the
future judgment, the reward of the good, the punishment of the
evil,—all to be regulated by righteous judgment; and having
given him all this information plainly and sufficiently, He de-
parted again to the invisible abodes. But while Abraham was still    3
in ignorance, as we said to you before, two sons were born to
him, of whom the one was called Ismael, and the other Helies-
dros. From the one are descended the barbarous nations, from
the other the people of the Persians, some of whom have adopted    4
the manner of living and the institutions of their neighbours, the
Brachmans. Others settled in Arabia, of whose posterity some
also have spread into Egypt. From them some of the Indians and    5
of the Egyptians have learned to be circumcised, and to be of
purer observance than others, although in process of time most of
them have turned to impiety what was the proof and sign of
purity.

## CHAP. 34—THE ISRAELITES IN EGYPT.

"Nevertheless, as he had got these two sons during the time    1
while he still lived in ignorance of things, having received the
knowledge of God, he asked of the Righteous One that he might
merit to have offspring by Sarah, who was his lawful wife, though
she was barren. She obtained a son, whom he named Isaac, from    2
whom came Jacob, and from him the twelve patriarchs, and from
these twelve seventy-two. These, when famine befell, came into    3
Egypt with all their family; and in the course of four hundred

years, being multiplied by the blessing and promise of God, they
4    were afflicted by the Egyptians. And when they were afflicted the
true Prophet appeared to Moses, and struck the Egyptians with
ten plagues, when they refused to let the Hebrew people depart
from them, and return to their native land; and he brought the
5    people of God out of Egypt. But those of the Egyptians who
survived the plagues, being infected with the animosity of their
6    king, pursued after the Hebrews. And when they had overtaken
them at the sea-shore, and thought to destroy and exterminate
them all, Moses, pouring out prayer to God, divided the sea into
two parts, so that the water was held on the right hand and on the
left as if it had been frozen, and the people of God passed as over
a dry road; but the Egyptians who were pursuing them, rashly
7    entering, were drowned. For when the last of the Hebrews came
out, the last of the Egyptians went down into the sea; and
straightway the waters of the sea, which by his command were
held bound as with frost, were loosed by his command who had
bound them, and recovering their natural freedom, inflicted
punishment on the wicked nation.

## CHAP. 35—THE EXODUS.

1        "After this, Moses, by the command of God, whose providence is over all, led out the people of the Hebrews into the
wilderness; and, leaving the shortest road which leads from
Egypt to Judaea, he led the people through long windings of the
wilderness, that, by the discipline of forty years, the novelty of a
changed manner of life might root out the evils which had clung to
them by a long-continued familiarity with the customs of the
2    Egyptians. Meantime they came to Mount Sinai, and thence the
law was given to them with voices and sights from heaven, written in ten precepts, of which the first and greatest was that they
should worship God Himself alone, and not make to themselves
3    any appearance or form to worship. But when Moses had gone up
to the mount, and was staying there forty days, the people, although they had seen Egypt struck with the ten plagues, and the

sea parted and passed over by them on foot, manna also given to them from heaven for bread, and drink supplied to them out of the rock that followed them, which kind of food was turned into whatever taste any one desired; and although, being placed under 4 the torrid region of heaven, they were shaded by a cloud in the day-time, that they might not be scorched by the heat, and by night were enlightened by a pillar of fire, lest the horror of darkness should be added to the wasteness of the wilderness;—those 5 very people, I say, when Moses stayed in the mount, made and worshipped a golden calf's head, after the fashion of Apis, whom they had seen worshipped in Egypt; and after so many and so great marvels which they had seen, were unable to cleanse and wash out from themselves the defilements of old habit. On this 6 account, leaving the short road which leads from Egypt to Judaea, Moses conducted them by an immense circuit of the desert, if haply he might be able, as we mentioned before, to shake off the evils of old habit by the change of a new education.

## CHAP. 36—ALLOWANCE OF SACRIFICE FOR A TIME.

"When meantime Moses, that faithful and wise steward, per- 1 ceived that the vice of sacrificing to idols had been deeply in- grained into the people from their association with the Egyptians, and that the root of this evil could not be extracted from them, he allowed them indeed to sacrifice, but permitted it to be done only to God, that by any means he might cut off one half of the deeply ingrained evil, leaving the other half to be corrected by another, and at a future time; by Him, namely, concerning whom he said himself, 'A prophet shall the Lord your God raise unto you, 2 whom ye shall hear even as myself, according to all things which He shall say to you. Whosoever shall not hear that prophet, his soul shall be cut off from his people.'

## CHAP. 37—THE HOLY PLACE.

1    "In addition to these things, he also appointed a place in
2  which alone it should be lawful to them to sacrifice to God. And
all this was arranged with this view, that when the fitting time
should come, and they should learn by means of the Prophet that
God desires mercy and not sacrifice, they might see Him who
should teach them that the place chosen of God, in which it was
suitable that victims should be offered to God, is his Wisdom; and
that on the other hand they might hear that this place, which
seemed chosen for a time, often harassed as it had been by hostile
invasions and plunderings, was at last to be wholly destroyed.
3  And in order to impress this upon them, even before the coming
of the true Prophet, who was to reject at once the sacrifices and
the place, it was often plundered by enemies and burnt with fire,
4  and the people carried into captivity among foreign nations, and
then brought back when they betook themselves to the mercy of
God; that by these things they might be taught that a people who
offer sacrifices are driven away and delivered up into the hands of
the enemy, but they who do mercy and righteousness are without
sacrifices freed from captivity, and restored to their native land.
5  But it fell out that very few understood this; for the greater
number, though they could perceive and observe these things, yet
were held by the irrational opinion of the vulgar: for right opinion
with liberty is the prerogative of a few.

## CHAP. 38—SINS OF THE ISRAELITES.

1    "Moses, then, having arranged these things, and having set
over the people one Auses to bring them to the land of their
fathers, himself by the command of the living God went up to a
2  certain mountain, and there died. Yet such was the manner of his
3  death, that till this day no one has found his burial-place. When,
therefore, the people reached their fathers' land, by the providence of God, at their first onset the inhabitants of wicked races
are routed, and they enter upon their paternal inheritance, which
4  was distributed among them by lot. For some time thereafter they
were ruled not by kings, but judges, and remained in a somewhat

peaceful condition. But when they sought for themselves tyrants 5
rather than kings, then also with regal ambition they erected a
temple in the place which had been appointed to them for prayer;
and thus, through a succession of wicked kings, the people fell
away to greater and still greater impiety.

## CHAP. 39—BAPTISM INSTITUTED IN PLACE OF SACRIFICES.

"But when the time began to draw near that what was want- 1
ing in the Mosaic institutions should be supplied, as we have said,
and that the Prophet should appear, of whom he had foretold that
He should warn them by the mercy of God to cease from sacrificing; lest haply they might suppose that on the cessation of sac- 2
rifice there was no remission of sins for them, He instituted baptism by water amongst them, in which they might be absolved
from all their sins on the invocation of His name, and for the
future, following a perfect life, might abide in immorality, being
purified not by the blood of beasts, but by the purification of the
Wisdom of God. Subsequently also an evident proof of this great 3
mystery is supplied *in the fact*, that every one who, believing in
this Prophet who had been foretold by Moses, is baptized in His
name, shall be kept unhurt from the destruction of war which
impends over the unbelieving nation, and the place itself; but that
those who do not believe shall be made exiles from their place and
kingdom, that even against their will they may understand and
obey the will of God.

## CHAP. 40—ADVENT OF THE TRUE PROPHET.

"These things therefore having been forearranged, He who 1
was expected comes, bringing signs and miracles as His creden-
tials by which He should be made manifest. But not even so did 2
the people believe, though they had been trained during so many
ages to the belief of these things. And not only did they not
believe, but they added blasphemy to unbelief, saying that He
was a gluttonous man and a belly-slave, and that He was actuated
by a demon, even He who had come for their salvation. To such 3
an extent does wickedness prevail by the agency of evil ones; so

that, but for the Wisdom of God assisting those who love the truth, almost all would have been involved in impious delusion.
4   Therefore He chose us twelve, the first who believed in Him, whom He named apostles; and afterwards other seventy-two most approved disciples, that, at least in this way recognising the pattern of Moses, the multitude might believe that this is He of whom Moses foretold, the Prophet that was to come.

## CHAP. 41—REJECTION OF THE TRUE PROPHET.

1       "But some one perhaps may say that it is possible for any one to imitate a number; but what shall we say of the signs and miracles which He wrought? For Moses had wrought miracles and
2   cures in Egypt. He also of whom he foretold that He should rise up a prophet like unto himself, though He cured every sickness and infirmity among the people, wrought innumerable miracles, and preached eternal life, was hurried by wicked men to the
3   cross; which deed was, however, by His power turned to good. In short, while He was suffering, all the world suffered with Him; for the sun was darkened, the mountains were torn asunder, the graves were opened, the veil of the temple was rent, as in lamen-
4   tation for the destruction impending over the place. And yet, though all the world was moved, they themselves are not even now moved to the consideration of these so great things.

## CHAP. 42—CALL OF THE GENTILES.

1       "But inasmuch as it was necessary that the Gentiles should be called into the room of those who remained unbelieving, so that the number might be filled up which had been shown to Abraham, the preaching of the blessed kingdom of God is sent
2   into all the world. On this account worldly spirits are disturbed, who always oppose those who are in quest of liberty, and who make use of the engines of error to destroy God's building; while those who press on to the glory of safety and liberty, being rendered braver by their resistance to these spirits, and by the toil of

great struggles against them, attain the crown of safety not without the palm of victory. Meantime, when He had suffered, 3 and darkness had overwhelmed the world from the sixth even to the ninth hour, as soon as the sun shone out again, and things were returned to their usual course, even wicked men returned to themselves and their former practices, their fear having abated. For some of them, watching the place with all care, when they 4 could not prevent His rising again, said that He was a magician; others pretended that He was stolen away.

## CHAP. 43—SUCCESS OF THE GOSPEL.

"Nevertheless, the truth everywhere prevailed; for, in proof 1 that these things were done by divine power, we who had been very few became in the course of a few days, by the help of God, far more than they. So that the priests at one time were afraid, lest haply, by the providence of God, to their confusion, the whole of the people should come over to our faith. Therefore they often sent to us, and asked us to discourse to them concerning Jesus, whether He were the Prophet whom Moses foretold, who is the eternal Christ. For on this point only does there seem to be any 2 difference between us who believe in Jesus, and the unbelieving Jews. But while they often made such requests to us, and we 3 sought for a fitting opportunity, a week of years was completed from the passion of the Lord, the Church of the Lord which was constituted in Jerusalem was most plentifully multiplied and grew, being governed with most righteous ordinances by James, who was ordained bishop in it by the Lord.

## CHAP. 44—CHALLENGE BY CAIAPHAS.

"But when we twelve apostles, on the day of the passover, 1 had come together with an immense multitude, and entered into the church of the brethren, each one of us, at the request of James, stated briefly, in the hearing of the people, what we had done in every place. While this was going on, Caiaphas, the high 2 priest, sent priests to us, and asked us to come to him, that either we should prove to him that Jesus is the eternal Christ, or he to us that He is not, and that so all the people should agree upon the one faith or the other; and this he frequently entreated us to do.

3 But we often put it off, always seeking for a more convenient time."

4 Then I, Clement, answered to this: "I think that this very question, whether He is the Christ, is of great importance for the establishment of the faith; otherwise the high priest would not so frequently ask that he might either learn or teach concerning the Christ."

5 Then Peter: "You have answered rightly, O Clement; for as no one can see without eyes, nor hear without ears, nor smell without nostrils, nor taste without a tongue, nor handle anything without hands, so it is impossible, without the true Prophet, to know what is pleasing to God."

6 And I answered: "I have already learned from your instruction that this true prophet is the Christ; but I should wish to learn what *the Christ* means, or why He is so called, that a matter of so great importance may not be vague and uncertain to me."

## CHAP. 45—THE TRUE PROPHET: WHY CALLED THE CHRIST.

1 Then Peter began to instruct me in this manner: "When God had made the world, as Lord of the universe, He appointed chiefs over the several creatures, over the trees even, and the mountains, and the fountains, and the rivers, and all things which He had made, as we have told you; for it were too long to mention

2 them one by one. He set, therefore, an angel as chief over the angels, a spirit over the spirits, a star over the stars, a demon over the demons, a bird over the birds, a beast over the beasts, a serpent over the serpents, a fish over the fishes, a man over men,

3 who is Christ Jesus. But He is called *Christ* by a certain excellent rite of religion; for as there are certain names common to kings, as Arsaces among the Persians, Caesar among the Romans, Pharaoh among the Egyptians, so among the Jews a king is called *Christ*.

And the reason of this appellation is this: Although indeed He was 4
the Son of God, and the beginning of all things, He became man;
Him first God anointed with oil which was taken from the wood of
the tree of life: from that anointing therefore He is called *Christ*. 5
Thence, moreover, He Himself also, according to the appoint-
ment of His Father, anoints with similar oil every one of the pious
when they come to His kingdom, for their refreshment after their
labours, as having got over the difficulties of the way; so that their
light may shine, and being filled with the Holy Spirit, they may be
endowed with immortality. But it occurs to me that I have suffi- 6
ciently explained to you the whole nature of that branch from
which that ointment is taken.

## CHAP. 46—ANOINTING.

"But now also I shall, by a very short representation, recall 1
you to the recollection of all these things. In the present life, 2
Aaron, the first high priest, was anointed with a composition of
chrism, which was made after the pattern of that spiritual ointment of which we have spoken before. He was prince of the
people, and as a king received first-fruits and tribute from the
people, man by man; and having undertaken the office of judging
the people, he judged of things clean and things unclean. But if 3
any one else was anointed with the same ointment, as deriving
virtue from it, he became either king, or prophet, or priest. If, 4
then, this temporal grace, compounded by men, had such effi-
cacy, consider now how potent was that ointment extracted by
God from a branch of the tree of life, when that which was made
by men could confer so excellent dignities among men. For what 5
in the present age is more glorious than a prophet, more illustrious than a priest, more exalted than a king?"

## CHAP. 47—ADAM ANOINTED A PROPHET

To this I replied: "I remember, Peter, that you told me of the 1
first man that he was a prophet; but you did not say that he was 2

anointed. If then there be no prophet without anointing, how could the first man be a prophet, since he was not anointed?"
3 Then Peter, smiling, said: "If the first man prophesied, it is certain that he was also anointed. For although he who has recorded the law in his pages is silent as to his anointing, yet he has evi-
4 dently left us to understand these things. For as, if he had said that he was anointed, it would not be doubted that he was also a prophet, although it were not written in the law; so, since it is certain that he was a prophet, it is in like manner certain that he was also anointed, because without anointing he could not be a
5 prophet. But you should rather have said, If the chrism was compounded by Aaron, by the perfumer's art, how could the first man be anointed before Aaron's time, the arts of composition not yet
6 having been discovered?" Then I answered: "Do not misunderstand me, Peter; for I do not speak of that compounded ointment and temporal oil, but of that simple and eternal *ointment*, which you told me was made by God, after whose likeness you say that that other was compounded by men."

## CHAP. 48—THE TRUE PROPHET, A PRIEST.

1    Then Peter answered, with an appearance of indignation: "What! do you suppose, Clement, that all of us can know all
2 things before the time? But not to be drawn aside now from our proposed discourse, we shall at another time, when your progress is more manifest, explain these things more distinctly.
3    "Then, however, a priest or a prophet, being anointed with the compounded ointment, putting fire to the altar of God, was
4 held illustrious in all the world. But after Aaron, who was a priest, another is taken out of the waters. I do not speak of Moses, but of Him who, in the waters of baptism, was called by God His Son.
5 For it is Jesus who has put out, by the grace of baptism, that fire
6 which the priest kindled for sins; for, from the time when He appeared, the chrism has ceased, by which the priesthood or the prophetic or the kingly office was conferred.

## CHAP. 49—TWO COMINGS OF CHRIST.

"His coming, therefore, was predicted by Moses, who deliv- 1
ered the law of God to men; but by another also before him, as I
have already informed you. He therefore intimated that He 2
should come, humble indeed in His first coming, but glorious in
His second. And the first, indeed, has been already accom- 3
plished; since He has come and taught, and He, the Judge of all,
has been judged and slain. But at His second coming He shall 4
come to judge, and shall indeed condemn the wicked, but shall
take the pious into a share and association with Himself in His
kingdom. Now the faith of His second coming depends upon His 5
first. For the prophets—especially Jacob and Moses—spoke of
the first, but some also of the second. But the excellency of 6
prophecy is chiefly shown in this, that the prophets spoke not of
things to come, according to the sequence of things; otherwise
they might seem merely as wise men to have conjectured what the
sequence of things pointed out.

## CHAP. 50—HIS REJECTION BY THE JEWS.

"But what I say is this: It was to be expected that Christ 1
should be received by the Jews, to whom He came, and that they
should believe on Him who was expected for the salvation of the
people, according to the traditions of the fathers; but that the
Gentiles should be averse to Him, since neither promise nor announcement concerning Him had been made to them, and indeed
He had never been made known to them even by name. Yet the 2
prophets, contrary to the order and sequence of things, said that
He should be the expectation of the Gentiles, and not of the Jews.
And so it happened. For when He came, He was not at all ac- 3
knowledged by those who seemed to expect Him, in consequence
of the tradition of their ancestors; whereas those who had heard
nothing at all of Him, both believe that He has come, and hope
that He is to come. And thus in all things prophecy appears faith- 4
ful, which said that He was the expectation of the Gentiles. The 5

Jews, therefore, have erred concerning the first coming of the
6 Lord; and on this point only there is disagreement betwixt us and
them. For they themselves know and expect that Christ shall
come; but that He has come already in humility—even He who is
7 called Jesus—they do not know. And this is a great confirmation
of His coming, that all do not believe on Him.

## CHAP. 51 —THE ONLY SAVIOUR.

1      "Him, therefore, has God appointed in the end of the world;
because it was impossible that the evils of men could be removed
by any other, provided that the nature of the human race were to
2 remain entire, i.e., the liberty of the will being preserved. This
condition, therefore, being preserved inviolate, He came to invite
to His kingdom all righteous ones, and those who have been
desirous to please Him. For these He has prepared unspeakable
good things, and the heavenly city Jerusalem, which shall shine
above the brightness of the sun, for the habitation of the saints.
3 But the unrighteous, and the wicked, and those who have de-
spised God, and have devoted the life given them to diverse wick-
ednesses, and have given to the practice of evil the time which
was given them for the work of righteousness, He shall hand over
4 to fitting and condign vengeance. But the rest of the things which
shall then be done, it is neither in the power of angels nor of men
to tell or to describe. This only it is enough for us to know, that
God shall confer upon the good an eternal possession of good
things."

## CHAP. 52—THE SAINTS BEFORE CHRIST'S COMING.

1      When he had thus spoken, I answered: "If those shall enjoy
the kingdom of Christ, whom His coming shall find righteous,
shall then those be wholly deprived of the kingdom who have died
2 before His coming?" Then Peter says: "You compel me, O Clement, to touch upon things that are unspeakable. But so far as it is
3 allowed to declare them, I shall not shrink from doing so. Know

then that Christ, who was from the beginning, and always, was ever present with the pious, though secretly, through all their generations; expecially with those who waited for Him, to whom He frequently appeared. But the time was not yet that there 4 should be a resurrection of the bodies that were dissolved; but this seemed rather to be their reward from God, that whoever should be found righteous, should remain longer in the body; or, at least, as is clearly related in the writings of the law concerning 5 a certain righteous man, that God translated him. In like manner others were dealt with, who pleased His will, that, being translated to Paradise, they should be kept for the kingdom. But as to those who have not been able completely to fulfil the rule of righteousness, but have had some remnants of evil in their flesh, their bodies are indeed dissolved, but their souls are kept in good and blessed abodes, that at the resurrection of the dead, when they shall recover their own bodies, purified even by the dissolution, they may obtain an eternal inheritance in proportion to their good deeds. And therefore blessed are all those who shall attain 6 to the kingdom of Christ; for not only shall they escape the pains of hell, but shall also remain incorruptible, and shall be the first to see God the Father, and shall obtain the rank of honour among the first in the presence of God.

## CHAP. 53 — ANIMOSITY OF THE JEWS.

"Wherefore there is not the least doubt concerning Christ; 1 and all the unbelieving Jews are stirred up with boundless rage against us, fearing lest haply He against whom they have sinned should be He. And their fear grows all the greater, because they 2 know that, as soon as they fixed Him on the cross, the whole world showed sympathy with Him; and that His body, although they guarded it with strict care, could nowhere be found; and that innumerable multitudes are attaching themselves to His faith. Whence they, together with the high priest Caiaphas, were com- 3 pelled to send to us again and again, that an inquiry might be instituted concerning the truth of His name. And when they were 4 constantly entreating that they might either learn or teach con-

cerning Jesus, whether He were the Christ, it seemed good to us to go up into the temple, and in the presence of all the people to bear witness concerning Him, and at the same time to charge the
5  Jews with many foolish things which they were doing. For the people was now divided into many parties, ever since the days of John the Baptist.

## Chap. 54—Jewish Sects.

1    "For when the rising of Christ was at hand for the abolition of sacrifices, and for the bestowal of the grace of baptism, the enemy, understanding from the predictions that the time was at hand, wrought various schisms among the people, that, if haply it might be possible to abolish the former sin, the latter fault might
2  be incorrigible. The first schism, therefore, was that of those who were called Sadducees, which took their rise almost in the time of John. These, as more righteous than others, began to separate themselves from the assembly of the people, and to deny the resurrection of the dead, and to assert that by an argument of infidelity, saying that it was unworthy that God should be worshipped, as it were, under the promise of a reward. The first
3  author of this opinion was Dositheus; the second was Simon.
4  Another schism is that of the Samaritans; for they deny the resurrection of the dead, and assert that God is not to be worshipped in
5  Jerusalem, but on Mount Gerizim. They indeed rightly, from the predictions of Moses, expect the one true Prophet; but by the wickedness of Dositheus they were hindered from believing that
6  Jesus is He whom they were expecting. The scribes also, and
7  Pharisees, are led away into another schism; but these, being baptized by John, and holding the word of truth received from the tradition of Moses as the key of the kingdom of heaven, have hid
8  it from the hearing of the people. Yea, some even of the disciples of John, who seemed to be great ones, have separated themselves from the people, and proclaimed their own master as the Christ.
9  But all these schisms have been prepared, that by means of them the faith of Christ and baptism might be hindered.

## Chap. 55 — Public Discussion.

"However, as we were proceeding to say, when the high 1
priest had often sent priests to ask us that we might discourse
with one another concerning Jesus; when it seemed a fit opportunity, and it pleased all the Church, we went up to the temple,
and, standing on the steps together with our faithful brethren, the 2
people kept perfect silence; and first the high priest began to
exhort the people that they should hear patiently and quietly, and
at the same time witness and judge of those things that were to be
spoken. Then, in the next place, exalting with many praises the 3
rite of sacrifice which had been bestowed by God upon the human
race for the remission of sins, he found fault with the baptism of
our Jesus, as having been recently brought in in opposition to the
sacrifices. But Matthew, meeting his propositions, showed 4
clearly, that whosoever shall not obtain the baptism of Jesus shall
not only be deprived of the kingdom of heaven, but shall not be
without peril at the resurrection of the dead, even though he be
fortified by the prerogative of a good life and an upright disposi-
tion. Having made these and such like statements, Matthew
stopped.

## Chap. 56 — Sadducees Refuted.

"But the party of the Sadducees, who deny the resurrection 1
of the dead, were in a rage, so that one of them cried out from
amongst the people, saying that those greatly err who think that
the dead ever arise. In opposition to him, Andrew, my brother, 2
answering, declared that it is not an error, but the surest matter of
faith, that the dead rise, in accordance with the teaching of Him of
whom Moses foretold that He should come the true Prophet. 'Or 3
if,' says he, 'you do not think that this is He whom Moses
foretold, let this first be inquired into, so that when this is clearly
proved to be He, there may be no further doubt concerning the
things which He taught.' These, and many such like things, Andrew proclaimed, and then stopped.

## CHAP. 57—SAMARITAN REFUTED.

1    "But a certain Samaritan, speaking against the people and against God, and asserting that neither are the dead to rise, nor is that worship of God to be maintained which is in Jerusalem, but that Mount Gerizim is to be reverenced, added also this in opposition to us, that our Jesus was not He whom Moses foretold as a
2    Prophet to come into the world. Against him, and another who supported him in what he said, James and John, the sons of
3    Zebedee, strove vigorously; and although they had a command not to enter into their cities, nor to bring the word of preaching to them, yet, lest their discourse, unless it were confuted, should hurt the faith of others, they replied so prudently and so power-
4    fully, that they put them to perpetual silence. For James made an oration concerning the resurrection of the dead, with the approbation of all the people; while John showed that if they would abandon the error of Mount Gerizim, they should consequently acknowledge that Jesus was indeed He who, according to the
5    prophecy of Moses, was expected to come; since, indeed, as Moses wrought signs and miracles, so also did Jesus. And there is no doubt but that the likeness of the signs proves Him to be that prophet of whom he said that He should come, 'like himself.' Having declared these things, and more to the same effect, they ceased.

## CHAP. 58—SCRIBES REFUTED.

1    "And, behold, one of the scribes, shouting out from the midst of the people, says: 'The signs and miracles which your Jesus
2    wrought, he wrought not as a prophet, but as a magician.' Him Philip eagerly encounters, showing that by this argument he ac-
3    cused Moses also. For when Moses wrought signs and miracles in Egypt, in like manner as Jesus also did in Judaea. it cannot be doubted that what was said of Jesus might as well be said of Moses. Having made these and such like protestations, Philip was silent.

## Chap. 59—Pharisees Refuted.

"Then a certain Pharisee, hearing this, chid Philip because he 1
put Jesus on a level with Moses. To whom Bartholomew, answer- 2
ing, boldly declared that we do not only say that Jesus was equal
to Moses, but that He was greater than he, because Moses was 3
indeed a prophet, as Jesus was also, but that Moses was not the
Christ, as Jesus was, and therefore He is doubtless greater who is
both a prophet and the Christ, than he who is only a prophet.
After following out this train of argument, he stopped. After him 4
James the son of Alphaeus gave an address to the people, with the
view of showing that we are not to believe in Jesus on the ground
that the prophets foretold concerning Him, but rather that we are
to believe the prophets, that they were really prophets, because
the Christ bears testimony to them; for it is the presence and 5
coming of Christ that show that they are truly prophets: for tes- 6
timony must be borne by the superior to his inferiors, not by the
inferiors to their superior. After these and many similar statements, James also was silent. After him Lebbaeus began vehe- 7
mently to charge it upon the people that they did not believe in
Jesus, who had done them so much good by teaching them the
things that are of God, by comforting the afflicted, healing the
sick, relieving the poor; yet for all these benefits their return had
been hatred and death. When he had declared these and many
more such things to the people, he ceased.

## Chap. 60—Disciples of John Refuted.

"And, behold, one of the disciples of John asserted that John 1
was the Christ, and not Jesus, inasmuch as Jesus Himself declared that John was greater than all men and all prophets. 'If, 2
then,' said he, 'he be greater than all, he must be held to be greater
than Moses, and than Jesus himself. But if he be the greatest of 3
all, then must he be the Christ.' To this Simon the Canaanite,
answering, asserted that John was indeed greater than all the

prophets, and all who are born of women, yet that he is not greater than the Son of man. Accordingly Jesus is also the Christ, whereas John is only a prophet: and there is as much difference between him and Jesus, as between the forerunner and Him whose forerunner he is; or as between Him who gives the law, and him who keeps the law. Having made these and similar statements, the Canaanite also was silent. After him Barnabas, who also is called Matthias, who was substituted as an apostle in the place of Judas, began to exhort the people that they should not regard Jesus with hatred, nor speak evil of Him. For it were far more proper, even for one who might be in ignorance or in doubt concerning Jesus, to love than to hate Him. For God has affixed a reward to love, a penalty to hatred. 'For the very fact,' said he, 'that He assumed a Jewish body, and was born among the Jews, how has not this incited us all to love Him?' When he had spoken this, and more to the same effect, he stopped.

## CHAP. 61 — CAIAPHAS ANSWERED.

1    "Then Caiaphas attempted to impugn the doctrine of Jesus,
2    saying that He spoke vain things, for He said that the poor are blessed; and promised earthly rewards; and placed the chief gift in an earthly inheritance; and promised that those who maintain righteousness shall be satisfied with meat and drink; and many
3    things of this sort He is charged with teaching. Thomas, in reply, proves that his accusation is frivolous; showing that the prophets, in whom Caiaphas believes, taught these things much more, and did not show in what manner these things are to be, or how they are to be understood; whereas Jesus pointed out how they are to be taken. And when he had spoken these things, and others of like kind, Thomas also held his peace.

## CHAP. 62 — FOOLISHNESS OF PREACHING.

1    "Therefore Caiaphas, again looking at me, and sometimes in the way of warning and sometimes in that of accusation, said that

I ought for the future to refrain from preaching Christ Jesus, lest I should do it to my own destruction, and lest, being deceived myself, I should also deceive others. Then, moreover, he charged 2 me with presumption, because, though I was unlearned, a fisherman, and a rustic, I dared to assume the office of a teacher. As he 3 spoke these things, and many more of like kind, I said in reply, that I incurred less danger, if, as he said, this Jesus were not the Christ, because I received Him as a teacher of the law; but that he was in terrible danger if this be the very Christ, as assuredly He is: for I believe in Him who has appeared; but for whom else, who 4 has never appeared, does he reserve his faith? But if I, an un- 5 learned and uneducated man, as you say, a fisherman and a rustic, have more understanding than wise elders, this, said I, ought the more to strike terror into you. For if I disputed with any 6 learning, and won over you wise and learned men, it would appear that I had acquired this power by long learning, and not by the grace of divine power; but now, when, as I have said, we 7 unskilled men convince and overcome you wise men, who that has any sense does not perceive that this is not a work of human subtlety, but of divine will and gift?

## CHAP. 63 — APPEAL TO THE JEWS.

"Thus we argued and bore witness; and we who were un- 1 learned men and fishermen, taught the priests concerning the one only God of heaven; the Sadducees, concerning the resurrection of the dead; the Samaritans, concerning the sacredness of Jerusalem (not that we entered into their cities, but disputed with them in public); the scribes and Pharisees, concerning the kingdom of heaven; the disciples of John, that they should not suffer John to be a stumbling-block to them; and all the people, that Jesus is the eternal Christ. At last, however, I warned them, that 2 before we should go forth to the Gentiles, to preach to them the knowledge of God the Father, they should themselves be reconciled to God, receiving His Son; for I showed them that in no way 3 else could they be saved, unless through the grace of the Holy Spirit they hasted to be washed with the baptism of threefold

4    invocation, and received the Eucharist of Christ the Lord, whom alone they ought to believe concerning those things which He taught, that so they might merit to attain eternal salvation; but that otherwise it was utterly impossible for them to be reconciled to God, even if they should kindle a thousand altars and a thousand high altars to Him.

## CHAP. 64 — TEMPLE TO BE DESTROYED.

1    " 'For we,' said I, 'have ascertained beyond doubt that God is much rather displeased with the sacrifices which you offer, the 2  time of sacrifices having now passed away; and because ye will not acknowledge that the time for offering victims is now past, therefore the temple shall be destroyed, and the abomination of desolation shall stand in the holy place; and then the Gospel shall be preached to the Gentiles for a testimony against you, that your 3  unbelief may be judged by their faith. For the whole world at different times suffers under divers maladies, either spreading generally over all, or affecting specially. Therefore it needs a 4  physician to visit it for its salvation. We therefore bear witness to you, and declare to you what has been hidden from every one of you. It is for you to consider what is for your advantage.'

## CHAP. 65 — TUMULT STILLED BY GAMALIEL.

1    "When I had thus spoken, the whole multitude of the priests were in a rage, because I had foretold to them the overthrow of 2  the temple. Which when Gamaliel, a chief of the people, saw — who was secretly our brother in the faith, but by our advice remained among them — because they were greatly enraged and 3  moved with intense fury against us, he stood up, and said, 'Be quiet for a little, O men of Israel, for ye do not perceive the trial which hangs over you. Wherefore refrain from these men; and if what they are engaged in be of human counsel, it will soon come to an end; but if it be from God, why will you sin without cause, and prevail nothing? For who can overpower the will of God?

Now therefore, since the day is declining towards evening, I shall   4
myself dispute with these men to-morrow, in this same place, in
your hearing, so that I may openly oppose and clearly confute
every error.' By this speech of his their fury was to some extent   5
checked, especially in the hope that next day we should be publicly convicted of error; and so he dismissed the people peace-
fully.

## CHAP. 66—DISCUSSION RESUMED.

"Now when we had come to our James, while we detailed to   1
him all that had been said and done, we supped, and remained
with him, spending the whole night in supplication to Almighty
God, that the discourse of the approaching disputation might
show the unquestionable truth of our faith. Therefore, on the   2
following day, James the bishop went up to the temple with us,
and with the whole church. There we found a great multitude,
who had been waiting for us from the middle of the night. There-   3
fore we took our stand in the same place as before, in order that,
standing on an elevation, we might be seen by all the people.
Then, when profound silence was obtained, Gamaliel, who, as we   4
have said, was of our faith, but who by a dispensation remained
amongst them, that if at any time they should attempt anything
unjust or wicked against us, he might either check them by skil-
fully adopted counsel, or might warn us, that we might either be
on our guard or might turn it aside;—he therefore, as if acting   5
against us, first of all looking to James the bishop, addressed him
in this manner:—

## CHAP. 67—SPEECH OF GAMALIEL.

"If I, Gamaliel, deem it no reproach either to my learning or   1
to my old age to learn something from babes and unlearned ones,
if haply there be anything which it is for profit or for safety to
acquire (for he who lives reasonably knows that nothing is more

precious than the soul), ought not this to be the object of love and desire to all, to learn what they do not know, and to teach what
2   they have learned? For it is most certain that neither friendship, nor kindred, nor lofty power, ought to be more precious to men
3   than truth. Therefore you, O brethren, if ye know anything more, shrink not from laying it before the people of God who are present, and also before your brethren; while the whole people shall
4   willingly and in perfect quietness hear what you say. For why should not the people do this, when they see even me equally with themselves willing to learn from you, if haply God has revealed
5   something further to you? But if you in anything are deficient, be not yet ashamed in like manner to be taught by us, that God may
6   fill up whatever is wanting on either side. But if any fear now agitates you on account of some of our people whose minds are prejudiced against you, and if through fear of their violence you dare not openly speak your sentiments, in order that I may deliver you from this fear, I openly swear to you by Almighty God who liveth for ever, that I will suffer no one to lay hands upon you.
7   Since, then, you have all this people witnesses of this, my oath, and you hold the covenant of our sacrament as a fitting pledge, let each one of you, without any hesitation, declare what he has learned; and let us, brethren, listen eagerly and in silence.'

## CHAP. 68—THE RULE OF FAITH.

1      "These sayings of Gamaliel did not much please Caiaphas; and holding him in suspicion, as it seemed, he began to insinuate
2   himself cunningly into the discussions: for, smiling at what Gamaliel had said, the chief of the priests asked of James, the chief of the bishops, that the discourse concerning Christ should not be drawn but from the Scriptures; 'that we may know,' said
3   he, 'whether Jesus be the very Christ or no.' Then said James, 'We must first inquire from what Scriptures we are especially to
4   derive our discussion.' Then he, with difficulty, at length overcome by reason, answered, that it must be derived from the law; and afterwards he made mention also of the prophets.

## Chap. 69—Two Comings of Christ.

"To him our James began to show, that whatsoever things   1
the prophets say they have taken from the law, and what they
have spoken is in accordance with the law. He also made some   2
statements respecting the books of the Kings, in what way, and
when, and by whom they were written, and how they ought to be
used. And when he had discussed most fully concerning the law,   3
and had, by a most clear exposition, brought into light whatever
things are in it concerning Christ, he showed by most abundant
proofs that Jesus is the Christ, and that in Him are fulfilled all the
prophecies which related to His humble advent. For he showed   4
that two advents of Him are foretold: one in humiliation, which
He has accomplished; the other in glory, which is hoped for to be
accomplished, when He shall come to give the kingdom to those
who believe in Him, and who observe all things which He has
commanded. And when he had plainly taught the people concern-   5
ing these things, he added this also: That unless a man be baptized
in water, in the name of the threefold blessedness, as the true
Prophet taught, he can neither receive remission of sins nor enter
into the kingdom of heaven; and he declared that this is the prescription of the unbegotten God. To which he added this also: 'Do   6
not think that we speak of two unbegotten Gods, or that one is
divided into two, or that the same is made male and female. But   7
we speak of the only-begotten Son of God, not sprung from another source, but ineffably self-originated; and in like manner we
speak of the Paraclete.' But when he had spoken some things also   8
concerning baptism, through seven successive days he persuaded
all the people and the high priest that they should hasten straightway to receive baptism.

## Chap. 70—Tumult Raised by Saul.

"And when matters were at that point that they should come   1
and be baptized, some one of our enemies, entering the temple
with a few men, began to cry out, and to say, 'What mean ye, O   2

men of Israel? Why are you so easily hurried on? Why are ye led headlong by most miserable men, who are deceived by Simon, a
3  magician?' While he was thus speaking, and adding more to the same effect, and while James the bishop was refuting him, he began to excite the people and to raise a tumult, so that the people
4  might not be able to hear what was said. Therefore he began to drive all into confusion with shouting, and to undo what had been arranged with much labour, and at the same time to reproach the priests, and to enrage them with revilings and abuse, and, like a
5  madman, to excite every one to murder, saying, 'What do ye? Why do ye hesitate? Oh, sluggish and inert, why do we not lay
6  hands upon them, and pull all these fellows to pieces?' When he had said this, he first, seizing a strong brand from the altar, set the
7  example of smiting. Then others also, seeing him, were carried
8  away with like madness. Then ensued a tumult on either side, of the beating and the beaten. Much blood is shed; there is a confused flight, in the midst of which that enemy attacked James, and threw him headlong from the top of the steps; and supposing him to be dead, he cared not to inflict further violence upon him.

## CHAP. 71—FLIGHT TO JERICHO.

1     "But our friends lifted him up, for they were both more numerous and more powerful than the others; but, from their fear of God, they rather suffered themselves to be killed by an inferior
2  force, than they would kill others. But when the evening came the priests shut up the temple, and we returned to the house of James, and spent the night there in prayer. Then before daylight
3  we went down to Jericho, to the number of 5,000 men. Then after three days one of the brethren came to us from Gamaliel, whom we mentioned before, bringing to us secret tidings that that enemy had received a commission from Caiaphas, the chief
4  priest, that he should arrest all who believed in Jesus, and should go to Damascus with his letters, and that there also, employing the help of the unbelievers, he should make havoc among the faithful; and that he was hastening to Damascus chiefly on this
5  account, because he believed that Peter had fled thither. And

about thirty days thereafter he stopped on his way while passing through Jericho going to Damascus. At that time we were absent, having gone out to the sepulchres of two brethren which were whitened of themselves every year, by which miracle the fury of   6 many against us was restrained, because they saw that our brethren were had in remembrance before God."